Civil Liability of Law Enforcement Officers

Civil Liability of Law Enforcement Officers

By

JOYCE BLALOCK

LL.M., Columbia University School of Law
LL.B., University of Denver College of Law
B.A., University of Texas
Agency Assistant Attorney General, New Mexico State Police
Member Bar of Commonwealth of Massachusetts
Member Bar of State of New Mexico

CHARLES C THOMAS • PUBLISHER
Springfield • Illinois • U.S.A.

Published and Distributed Throughout the World by

CHARLES C THOMAS • PUBLISHER
Bannerstone House
301-327 East Lawrence Avenue, Springfield, Illinois, U.S.A.

ISBN 0-398-02864-8

Library of Congress Catalog Card Number: 73-4778

With THOMAS BOOKS careful attention is given to all details of manufacturing and design. It is the Publisher's desire to present books that are satisfactory as to their physical qualities and artistic possibilities and appropriate for their particular use. THOMAS BOOKS will be true to those laws of quality that assure a good name and good will.

Printed in the United States of America
R-1

Library of Congress Cataloging in Publication Data

Blalock, Joyce.
Civil liability of law enforcement officers.
1. Tort liability of the police—United States.
2. Government liability——United States. I. Title.
KF1307.B56 346'.73'033 73-4778
ISBN 0-398-02864-8

TO

The New Mexico State Police

PREFACE

ACCUSATIONS of false arrest, unnecessary force, improper training and deprivation of constitutional rights emerge as an epidemic of lawsuits against patrolmen, supervisors, jailers, prison officials, private police and National Guardsmen. Plaintiffs revamp the old charges into winning claims. Defenses that have prevailed no longer guarantee verdicts for officer-defendants. Times have changed; law enforcers are sued; some are held liable.

This rash of suits is no isolated phenomenon. In all fields, the phrase "I'll sue you" moves from threat to reality. Immunities of governments and charities are being abolished. Medical malpractice cases – almost unheard of a few years ago – increase in doctor-frightening numbers. Products liability complaints naming car manufacturers, medicine producers and food companies crowd the dockets. Consumer litigation and indigent cases expand the remedies. The year of the rat, the age of aquarius and the era of the courtroom have arrived.

How can an individual gauge his risk of liability? One way is to examine court decisions. Cases arise from conflicts. Citizen X states that Officer Y negligently shot him, causing injuries of $50,000. Y contends that the shot was justified by X's actions. Each testifies to the facts as he knows them. Legal doctrines translate these facts into rights and duties concluding with either a fixed sum of money or no damages. Recovery is based upon actual losses and the deviation by defendant from the legal standard of conduct. Such a holding demonstrates that particular facts did or did not result in liability. This narrow ruling is fitted into the pattern of other decisions to define general law governing the use of weapons. Although federal codes, state statutes and municipal ordinances vary, cases in New York, California and Illinois must be read to evaluate local judgments and to focus on developing trends. Of course, opinions of the United States Supreme Court are of especial significance in formulating the rules of law in all jurisdictions.

In addition to allegations that raise the spectre of financial loss, other complaints affect law enforcers. Officers, organizations and governmental units are ordered to refrain from some methods of arrest or are required to allow constitutional rights to prisoners. Judges, remote from street encounters and prison conflagrations, decree guidelines enforceable by contempt of court.

Agencies and legislators react to the flood of lawsuits. Grievance procedures, civilian review boards and internal disciplinary measures are multiplying. Insurance coverage is prevalent. Immunity provisions absolve individuals and shift the burden to institutions.

Being a target for litigation is traumatic, but there are some positive spin-offs. Fear of liability curbs those who would misuse their powers. Respect for policemen and awareness of their dangerous assignment are evident in the exoneration of police defendants. Frivolous claims are quickly dismissed. Complaints mirror public expectations while the judicial spotlight illuminates how the law enforcer met the challenge. Most officers prove to court and jury that they acted reasonably. The ones who cannot live up to their awesome responsibilities suffer in order that departments will maintain high standards.

This book explores basic theories of liability, categories of potential defendants, situations which generate controversies, effective defenses, suggestions for preventing complaints and departmental controls. The law and the direction of its movement are discussed. By studying incidents which have led to damages and probing valid defenses, law enforcers can learn the techniques of liability-avoidance.

JOYCE BLALOCK

ACKNOWLEDGMENTS

WITH appreciation I acknowledge the following;

To Professor Thompson Marsh, of the University of Denver College of Law, who taught me about rights and duties.

To Chief Martin E. Vigil, former Chief Joseph A. Black and the New Mexico State Police Board members, past and present, who have given me the opportunity to work in law enforcement.

To Robert J. Wirth, Special Agent, F. B. I., who has been an excellent source of information on law enforcement legal matters and their day-to-day application.

To Margaret W. Lamb for reviewing the manuscript and offering valuable comments.

To Barbara Whitlock for vital assistance with this book from its inception as words and ideas to the drudgery and excitement of its completion.

J. B.

CONTENTS

Chapter *Page*

PART THREE – ALTERNATIVES TO CIVIL LIABILITY

Civil Liability of Law Enforcement Officers

PART ONE...

WHO, WHAT, WHEN, WHERE AND WHY OF CIVIL LIABILITY

CHAPTER ONE

OVERVIEW OF CIVIL LITIGATION

LAW is as new as today's court decision and as old as man. Law is as stable as our two century old Constitution and as adaptable as a United States Supreme Court Opinion applying the Fourth Amendment to wiretapping.

Laws regulate activities from competitive prices of Fords to punishments for murder. The entire spectrum of living is touched. As expected with such a pervasive subject, law cannot be found in a neat pile of rules. There are countless bundles modified by additional stacks and overridden by others. The purpose of this chapter is to point out some of the sources of law and to highlight the legal process as it relates to civil litigation against officers.

The supreme law in America is the United States Constitution. State constitutions and statutes enacted by local, state or federal bodies can be struck down if they conflict with the Constitution. Judicial opinions at any level may be reversed if unconstitutional. The final authority to construe this document is the United States Supreme Court.

The Constitution was ratified in the late 1700's. Up to the present, only a few short amendments have been added to it. Examine this history alongside that of state constitutions. Many of them are hundreds of pages long and are replete with obsolete directives. Several states have completely rewritten their constitutions; the federal model stands with virtually no revision. The difference could be likened to comparing man with dinosaur. The former is small and adaptable; the latter was gross and lethargic.

A recent case by a prisoner against a warden illustrates the effect of the Constitution in civil cases. An inmate was ordered to sign a *safety sheet* which he believed to be a waiver of his right to sue the officials. He refused to sign. The deputy warden punished him with the severest penalty: confinement in a strip-cell under squalid and painful conditions. The warden was aware of these circumstances, and he testified that the treatment was inappropriate. *Held,* in a suit brought under the federal civil rights act, prisoner recovered damages from warden for violation of his rights under the Eighth Amendment of the United States Constitution (1).

The Eighth Amendment reads "Excessive bail shall not be required, nor excessive fines imposed, nor cruel and unusual punishment inflicted." To enforce such provisions and to curtail tyranny of the Ku Klux Klan, Congress in 1871 enacted the civil rights acts. They lay dormant for almost a hundred years until rediscovered in the 1960's. Today the two hundred year old protections, implemented by the one hundred year old statutes, fill the dockets in federal courts. Punishments adjudged cruel and unusual have had their evolution too. The fact that certain treatment of prisoners has been accepted does not mean that it will be tolerated now. The definition adjusts as the practices and expectations of society mature. Cases outline what constitutes cruel and unusual punishment. These decisions are law.

DEVELOPMENT OF AMERICAN LAW

Before continuing the discussion of American law, a review of the past is helpful. A page of history is worth a dozen pages of logic in reaching a perspective. This system evolved from the English common law in effect at the time of the American Revolution. Common law is derived from court opinions. Many subjects, such as civil assault and battery, are controlled by case law. These judge-made rules are found in decisions of the courts. Using judicial holdings as precedent, lawyers predict the judgment in new cases. Law has been defined as predictability.

Precedent is the goal of legal research. Attorneys seek cases from the local jurisdiction and elsewhere, that are similar to the problem at hand. Even though new inventions, for example in medicine and transportation, seem to separate current happenings from older events, principles remain the same. Doctrines

1. *Wright v. McMann,* 387 F.2d 519 (2nd Cir. 1967). Case is also discussed in Chapter Fifteen.

developed in the era of horse and buggy control Mustang and Coupe de Ville today. The reasoning flows from specific facts to a narrow holding; a pattern develops into a general rule. The latter standing alone is the skeleton that has no substance without the flesh of facts. The common law expands daily. Precedent incorporates social change. For example, early oil and gas law evolved from theories which determined the right to possess wild animals. Both mineral and animal were compared in discovery, flight and pursuit. Old methods are adaptable; astronauts explore the moon in four-wheeled vehicles.

Lawyers often discover appellate court decisions which match their client's case. These opinions are cited as precedent. When no earlier holding is exactly in point, attorneys argue that certain rulings are so close as to be controlling or are so remote as to be distinguishable. Reasoning by analogy, contentions build to the desired conclusion. Briefs are chock full of such language as *binding precedent, majority rule, recent trends* and *the better reasoning*. Law is an art, not a science.

Many kinds of lawsuits originated in common law. Usually personal injury remedies have arisen and evolved through individual cases. Statutes have not played a significant role in this development. First the outline of a general rule emerged from specific decisions, then subtle variations molded the principle to fit different circumstances. One notable exception is litigation initiated to recover for fatal wounds (wrongful death); this action was established by statute. At common law the harmed person could sue; however, the complaint was dismissed if he died. The unfairness of this doctrine led to legislation permitting others to sue on behalf of decedents and for their own losses resulting from the death.

Even when a theory of liability, such as negligence, is carved out of lawsuits, statutes govern procedures. Where (venue), in what court (jurisdiction), when (statute of limitations), against whom (defendant; respondent) and by whom (plaintiff; petitioner) are dictated by legislation and court rules. These are construed by judges. It is frequently said that no one can draft a law which is clear in all instances. Decisions interpreting statutes prove this true.

In most jurisdictions only the opinions of the highest court are published. Some states, such as Pennsylvania and New York, and federal districts disseminate trial level and intermediate appellate decisions. Unless these holdings have been reversed or modified, they also constitute precedent. In reality, precedent boils down to available materials. Unpublished decisions are not precedent. Of course, a judge is king in his tribunal and usually follows his former rulings. Individual magistrates can be independent arbiters of the law and lean toward one side: *hanging judges* or *plaintiffs judges.* Human prejudices and errors permeate lawsuits. An erroneous verdict may be reversed on appeal by either party in a civil case, but the process is lengthy, expensive and uncertain. Ordinarily civil litigation turns upon the money involved. Negotiations and settlements dog every stage.

Stability rests on courts following precedent. But, when the mores change, new doctrines emerge, or faulty reasoning is demonstrated, judges reverse former decisions. The dynamics of a flexible system spring from the tension of advocates who stress opposing arguments. Growth is as essential as permanence to a vital jurisprudence.

Many civil remedies are statutory: workmen's compensation and garnishment. Statutes spell out jurisdiction, the basis for a complaint and the relief. However, cases delineate which acts make up a violation, valid defenses and damages. Criminal law is almost entirely statutory. But, courts define *intent, reckless* and *malice.* Thus, the common law system in America includes numerous statutes and myriad decisions.

Administrative law expands to fill the gaps between courts and legislation. Public employees perform in accordance with departmental regulations. Treasury rulings control tax administration. Transportation moves pursuant to local department and interstate commerce commission directives. Civil rights commissions investigate police conduct. Federal and state agencies form part of the executive branch of government, subject to statutes of the legislature and holdings of the judiciary. Checks and balances are fundamental to American government.

TORT LAW

The portion of civil law designated as *torts* encompasses most personal injury litigation. A tort is a legal wrong committed upon a person or property independent of a contract. The phrase legal wrong must be kept in mind. Not all clashes are actionable in court. Many unpleasant contacts are adjudged as the give and take of man in society. Tort law is primarily a judicially developed system for awarding damages to the injured. The origin of this subject harks back to ancient needs to protect the peace and prevent self-help. The sovereign set up a forum for parties to prove their claims peacefully. Civil rights actions follow general tort theories and often allow remedies otherwise available in common law tort suits. For example, a claim of violation of the constitutional right to be free from unreasonable seizure may arise from facts which amount to the tort of false arrest.

A typical recent complaint alleging the tort of negligence is as follows: A police unit chased a person suspected of leaving the scene of an accident over a narrow, winding and wet road, in a residential section at speeds up to 100 m.p.h. The officer radioed for a roadblock. A fellow policeman aligned a squad car across the road 600 to 800 feet below the top of a steep hill. A taxi driver stopped at the roadblock. The fleeing motorist topped the hill at 90 m.p.h. and hit the unit and the taxi, killing the taxi driver. At the speeds of the chase, a vehicle could not have come over the hill and stopped in less than 1750 feet. *Held,* judgment against the two officers and municipality for creating an unreasonable risk to public safety (2).

Two general categories of torts, intentional torts and negligence, cover most of the petitions against law enforcers. The doctrine of fault is integral to both as can be seen from a listing of some effective defenses. For intentional torts, defenses are self-defense, privilege and consent. For negligence, respondents answer unavoidable accident, contributory negligence and sudden emergency. A complaint for the intentional tort of assault and battery during an arrest may be defeated by proof that the arrest was lawful and only reasonable force was used: a privilege. A winning defense to a suit grounded on a collision between a patrol unit and a truck would be establishing that the trucker's negligence contributed to cause the crash, even though the officer was negligent. A few

2. *Myers v. Town of Harrison,* 438 F.2d 293 (2nd Cir. 1971). Case is also discussed in Chapter Five.

states have modified contributory negligence into comparative negligence so that the degree of responsibility of the parties is weighed. Recovery goes to the person who was the least to blame and is in proportion to the differing amounts of negligence.

The idea of fault was borrowed from criminal law; it may be inappropriate to civil litigation. Like the element of intent in crime, fault is intangible. Either may be inferred from facts. The sum and kind of recovery often reflect the degree of fault. Compensatory damages repay injured persons for such losses as wages, medical bills and disabilities. These must be proven. Pain and suffering, also compensatory damages, are subjective items which are sometimes increased to adjudge fault. Punitive, or exemplary damages resemble fines in criminal law; they signify censure. Such damages are awarded only in extreme cases.

In negligence suits defendant will not be liable unless he foresaw, or should have anticipated, that his actions or omissions would imperil another. Foreseeability is evaluated from the vantage point of the reasonable man. In the case with the taxi driver, if a stowaway in the squad car were hurt, his injuries could not have been anticipated and he would lose in court. However, if the trooper, because of prior experience, were aware that stowaways might be in his unit, the danger was foreseeable whether or not the policeman actually thought of the matter at the time.

The actions or omissions of defendant must be the proximate cause of plaintiff's harm. There must be a direct relationship between what defendant did or failed to do and the damage to plaintiff. Such relationship exists when a jailer leaves a wounded prisoner in a cell without medical aid, and the inmate dies from treatable injuries. Independent, intervening causes can block liability. However, if defendant's negligence placed an individual in a hazardous situation from which harm resulted, defendant would be responsible. Defendant takes plaintiff as defendant finds him. That is, a person may recover for the full extent of his loss even though a healthy fellow similarly subjected to the negligence would have suffered virtually no injury.

Public policy, expressed in legislation, has removed some types of cases from the fault-tort arena: workmen's compensation claims. A ground swell of support for no-fault laws for automobile accidents exposes wide dissatisfaction with the handling of these complaints. Frequently parties do not file lawsuits because of insurance coverage or an aversion to litigation.

COMPARISON BETWEEN CRIMINAL AND CIVIL LAW

Criminal and civil law may be compared by discussing an actual case. In a bar late at night, plaintiff spoke derogatorily to an officer. Concluding that the fellow was drunk and disorderly, the angry policeman escorted him from the bar and told him to go home. He immediately reappeared. The officer threw him onto the pavement outside where he landed with such force that both bones of one leg were badly shattered. *Held,* in an assault and battery civil proceeding, the officer was liable (3).

This episode could have been the basis for criminal charges against the policeman as well as for civil damages. In the United States, a crime is an offense against the people. Fines revert to the treasury; incarceration of violators benefits the public. The usual civil relief is money, although some plaintiffs demand that respondents perform, or prohibit them from doing, specific activities. Neither criminal nor civil law encompasses all abuses of the public or suffering of the individual. Much of the abrasiveness in our society remains in the realm of morals.

The Fifth Amendment of the United States Constitution provides: " . . . nor shall any person be subject for the same offense to be twice in jeopardy of life or limb." The freedom is from two prosecutions for the same offense. It does not apply to the founding of both a criminal charge and a civil complaint on one incident. A single event may give rise to one criminal charge and any combination of civil remedies, such as a suit for damages, loss of license or termination of employment.

Another provision of the Fifth Amendment, " . . . nor shall be compelled in any Criminal Case to be a witness against himself," means that the accused may refuse to testify. The prosecutor cannot comment on the refusal. A civil defendant, or witness in

3. *Mead v. O'Connor,* 66 N.M. 170, 344 P.2d 478 (1959).

any trial, may claim the Fifth Amendment in response to a question; but, when subpoenaed to court, he cannot exercise his Fifth Amendment privilege by declining to take the witness stand. The *Miranda* warnings apply in criminal procedure as a necessary explanation to a suspect of his privilege against self-incrimination. Unless proper warnings are given, answers to inquiries are suppressable in court.

In a civil suit both sides have greater access to the evidence relied upon by the other party than in criminal trials. Court-ruled-discovery is fast developing in the criminal sphere; however, it is not as comprehensive as the civil tools of interrogatories, depositions and pretrial disclosures.

Other significant variations are the burden of proof borne by the plaintiff and the right to appeal. The burden of proof for the government is to establish all elements of the crime beyond a reasonable doubt. In civil litigation the burden of proof usually is by a preponderance of the evidence. The former is obviously more onerous than the latter. Preponderance of the evidence denotes only enough additional belief that plaintiff has established his case, beyond acceptance of the defense contentions, if any, to tip the scales in favor of plaintiff. Either party may appeal civil decisions. Defendants always may appeal criminal verdicts; however, the government has almost no right to appeal.

CONCLUSION

The American system combines new and old methods into a unique blend that is both innovative and stable. Fashioning law from cases may seem roundabout until it is seen that flexibility emerges from this ongoing process. In the inevitable lag between a changing society and a precedent oriented law, principles are developed before hardening into legalisms. When revisions are necessary, judges modify rules and legislators enact amendments. Meanwhile, cases reveal present law and aid in predictions about future litigation.

CHAPTER TWO

WHO GETS SUED?

PERSONS in the criminal justice system who may be liable fall into two general categories. One is the assaulting policemen or negligent guard. He is directly answerable for the harm caused by his conduct. In the other group are those, such as supervisors and agencies, connected indirectly with an incident.

The ordinary episodes which lead to liability of an officer are the one-to-one encounters in the alley, pursuits of violators or struggles at the lockup. An individual is accountable for his behavior. Usually he is not responsible for actions of others.

Allegations of negligent training or supervision multiply. Plaintiff has the burden of proving that defendant failed to properly execute a duty to train or supervise and that the harm resulted therefrom. The injury to plaintiff is transmitted through a third person, but the crux of the argument is the negligence of the commander.

Depending upon the facts, the supervisor may be either directly or indirectly accountable. A field commander, at the scene, could be immediately involved because he did not control a subordinate. Up the organization ladder, a chief's liability hinges upon failure to manage personnel so as to avoid the incident. Agency responsibility depends on similar principles.

Plaintiffs sue everyone who might be liable. When preparing pleadings, it is easy to add defendants. Judges discourage petitioners from including parties not clearly linked to the occurrence, although great leeway exists. By joining extra persons petitioners hope to negotiate better settlements or to broaden targets for damages. There is no effective deterrent to listing officers, commanders and departments. Those sued move for dismissal; if this motion is sustained, defendants rarely proceed against plaintiffs. Successful claims of abuse of process are uncommon.

After a riot, supervisors may be sued because the injured person is not sure who hurt him. Even with pictures, identification is confused by protective gear and gas masks. Participants have a Fifth Amendment right, privilege against self-incrimination, not to reveal themselves. Claims filed against *John Doe* must be dismissed if by the trial date no individual has been substituted to present his own defense and, if necessary, to pay damages.

In a recent civil rights case stemming from a demonstration at a university, the names of the National Guardsmen who inflicted wounds were unknown. Although the men had been photographed, the formation of the unit gave no clue to identity and all wore gas masks. None admitted the bayonneting. Plaintiffs obtained a list of the 88 Battery members. However, a motion was denied to join all 88, among whom were the two or three who apparently had used excessive force. Thus, the only respondents were high level commanders. Blame could not be tied to the governor. Generals, colonels and others of rank showed that training in the exercise of reasonable force had been adequate. The jury exonerated them from the acts of the Guardsmen (4).

In another case in which six unidentified federal narcotics agents searched an apartment, the dweller sued *six unknown agents* and then discovered their names through a court order for records disclosing who engaged in the raid. If their identity had remained secret, supervisors probably would have been sued (5).

New statutes give riot victims the right to collect from the government. These provisions distribute individual loss to the public. Usually there is a ceiling on recovery, but some relief is afforded to the innocent bystander. Similar laws recompense victims of crimes.

Auxiliary police stand in a position analogous to regular officers. Their responsibility is predicated upon similar doctrines. When performing as police, they are empowered as law enforcers.

4. *Dressman v. Cargo,* U.S.D.C. D.N.M., #8563 Civ. (1971).
5. *Bivens v. Six Unknown Named Agents of the Fed. Bur. of Narcotics,* 403 U.S. 388, 29 L. Ed. 2d 619, 91 S. Ct. 1999 (1971); on remand 456 F. 2d 1339 (2nd Cir. 1972). [see also Ch. 10]

Security guards and private investigators may hold licenses allowing them to serve their employers. Often they are also commissioned officers. Their liability may depend upon whether they were acting in a private or public capacity.

Sheriffs and their deputies have a legal status that is different from that of other law enforcers. Ordinarily, sheriffs are elected officials who appoint deputies as their agents, whereas a police chief or prison warden is an executive whose subordinates work for an organization. These employees meet civil service qualifications and are regulated in accordance with department standards. However, sheriffs direct and are responsible for acts of deputies. Archaic terms of master-servant characterize this relationship. By the case law of master-servant, the master is liable for acts of his servant. Legal control results in liability for injuries caused by the deputy.

Mutual aid agreements between agencies present tricky questions of responsibility. This may be set out in a contract, but the arrangement is not binding upon an injured citizen. He is not a party to the agreement. The defendant's remedy may be to join the department that has consented to absolve him and to sue it for breach of contract.

CONCLUSION

Who in the criminal justice system is subject to civil litigation? The answer is everyone. New remedies and adaptations of ancient theories spur plaintiffs to initiate suits. Just as employee and official are answerable to employer and public for job performance, they are now accountable to those whom they imperil.

CHAPTER THREE

TYPES OF LAWSUITS

A FEW years ago the typical suit against a law enforcer alleged misuse of force. While these complaints continue, new cases are generated from the total spectrum of criminal justice work. All kinds of citizen versus citizen tort contentions emerge in civilian-officer contexts. In addition, asserted deprivations of constitutional rights extend to most official dealings. Specific activities may be divided, for purposes of discussion, into conservation of the peace, intelligence functions, arrests, searches and incarceration. Most claims evolve from confrontations in these areas.

The term *conservation of the peace* covers a multitude of police business. Preventive measures, such as patrol and intervention in disputes, fit into this classification. A new focus is the mass demonstration. Attempts to quell incipient mob violence may lead to charges of violation of the First Amendment of the Constitution – freedom of speech and assembly – filed in federal court under the civil rights acts. These laws apply only to state and local officers, including National Guardsmen on duty for the state.

However, recent cases indicate that federal officers and political subdivisions also may be held responsible for deprivation of constitutional rights. Conspiracies to violate someone's privileges, as well as actual deprivations, are prohibited. Although money may be a goal, damages often are unascertainable. Petitioners sue to prevent the reoccurrence of particular responses or to stop anticipated conduct. A judgment enjoining the police from interfering with guaranteed rights is only a restatement of the law; rights exist and interference with their exercise is illegal. Such proceedings familiarize a court with the problem. If the injunction is violated, speedy relief from this forum will come through contempt powers.

Remedies obtainable by those aggrieved through intelligence operations are similar to the ones mentioned above. Plaintiffs allege invasion of privacy and attempt to stop further surveillance and information gathering. Objections to official dossiers mount. Newsmen unveil investigations of radicals who have no apparent criminal designs. Government photographers and agents intrude into the protest scene and infiltrate organizations. In the language of the United States Supreme Court, such activities have a chilling effect upon First Amendment rights to speak freely, to assemble and to issue news. Few people deny the need to amass data, but strong disapproval emerges as the material is unrelated to criminals and focuses on political questioners.

Police are not the only ones against whom there is an outcry of interference with privacy. Information trading practices in the commercial world are restricted by federal and state legislation. The doctrine of right to privacy was employed to void statutes prohibiting the sale of contraceptives. Libel and slander suits curb publication of derogatory statements by citizens and officials. Computer storage threatens access to details about everyone. Public indignation is aroused over possible misuses; government and private investigators are targets for this anxiety.

The law enforcement activity which generates the most litigation is the arrest. Insurance protection for police has been popularly entitled false arrest coverage. Most assault and battery claims arise from arrests. This is partly due to the inherent nature of an arrest. Also, a general practice prevails to arrest anyone against whom force is used, especially if the officer thinks that the person might file a complaint. Torts of assault and battery or false arrest and false imprisonment are pled as unreasonable seizure of the individual contrary to the Fourth Amendment.

Under the common law a person could resist an unlawful arrest or one in which the arrest authority was not clearly apparent. This privilege grew out of the practical result of an arrest. Many arrestees did not survive. No speedy arraignment required prompt appearance before a magistrate; bail and personal recognizance were unobtainable; jail conditions threatened physical well-being. Many states have abolished the common law of legally resisting arrest and have substituted a duty to submit. Remedies for illegal arrest, after the fact, usually are safer for everyone.

Others injured during an arrest are bystanders and those assisting the officer. They may be hurt or their property harmed. In many jurisdictions it is a crime not to aid a policeman when requested. The civilian faces a dilemma of helping at his peril or committing an offense. Courts are sympathetic to his plight and give him demanded relief. Injured bystanders usually recover if the officer was negligent.

An appellate court recently decided a civil rights appeal which may open a new field of litigation. A murder defendant was convicted in Illinois. Eight years later the Illinois supreme court reversed the conviction on the basis of an illegally obtained confession. Upon retrial, without the confession, defendant was acquitted. A federal civil suit was filed against the officers who coerced the confession. The trial court dismissed the complaint, but the dismissal was reversed upon appeal. The court held that plaintiff could not collect for the eight year prison stay, but he could recover for other damages flowing from the involuntary confession.

Plaintiff was a juvenile when arrested. For 18 days he remained in solitary confinement seeing neither family nor friends. Immediately thereafter, two officers took him into a room, handcuffed him to a chair, allegedly beat and threatened him while interrogating him for more than 22 hours. He signed a written confession of murder. Plaintiff asserted that defendants deprived him of life, liberty and property without due process of law in violation of the Fourteenth Amendment. He claimed bodily pain and injury, mental anguish, past and future loss of money by reason of his imprisonment. The court specified that plaintiff's recovery did not depend upon the presence of physical violence; proof of psychological coercion would suffice. This holding is significant both in giving civil rights relief to a person harmed by improper police procedure and in allowing a claim to be filed many years after the incident. As to the latter point, the court ruled that the statute of limitations was tolled while plaintiff was in prison (6). If other judges follow this decision, law enforcers

6. *Duncan v. Nelson,* 11 Cr. L. 2086 (7th Cir. 1972).

can expect a flood of new cases.

Searches give rise to complaints for property damage, as well as for personal injury. In criminal trials, technical rules interpreting the Fourth Amendment control the introduction into evidence of seized items. Motions to suppress illegally seized materials are routine. Contraband is not returnable even though improperly taken. Other articles must be handed back plus compensation for damage, including loss of use. Forced entry to premises may injure an innocent party. For example, landlords and motel owners ordinarily are not involved in refusals of peaceful entry. Such persons collect for harm to premises during searches.

Impoundment of vehicles leads to many claims of property loss. In some judicial districts articles found during a car inventory are not legally obtained evidence for a criminal prosecution. These courts require a search warrant. Thus, the patrolman chooses between securing legal evidence and an inventory for his protection against charges of theft. Other jurisdictions take a realistic view and permit reasonable inventories which are standard practice of the department. It is desirable to inventory in the presence of the person in control of the vehicle and to have him sign his approval. Later complaints of missing items should be forestalled by these tactics. But often such persons will be drunk or otherwise incompetent to witness the inventory, or necessity will dictate their immediate incarceration.

Complaints of misappropriation of property are also made after searches of homes. Articles not listed on the search warrant inventory are said to have been taken. Warrantless searches of persons and property also give rise to such charges. Usually articles removed from a prisoner during booking are listed on a receipt and are thus accounted for to everyone's satisfaction.

The tort of conversion is alleged for exerting control over the property of another. Damages may amount to the total value of the goods, in effect a forced sale to defendant. For minor interferences with the owner's interest, recovery is limited to loss of use and actual harm.

Trespass is another property claim. The injury ordinarily is minimal and damages are nominal. Therefore, a suit based on trespass alone is infrequently filed, although it might be included along with other counts such as invasion of privacy or defamation of character. Sheriffs and their deputies are especially susceptible to such claims when they execute a judgment or seize property under civil process. Commission of a tort during such procedure turns an initial lawful entry into a trespass.

A big category of lawsuits which cuts across every activity is negligence. It can arise from any careless action. Most motor vehicle cases are based upon negligence. Also, complaints founded on failure to act generally are so pled. The ground for this charge is an unfulfilled duty to act and a showing that the duty is owed to the individual harmed. Dereliction of duty does not apply only to public officers. Clients of private security forces also win verdicts for this tort. In such cases it is easier than with a public official for plaintiff to prove that the duty is owed to him.

Cases pressing for rights or prisoners are a bursting field of litigation. Until recently most inmate claims related to strong-arm tactics. Now the clamor is for constitutional rights. Prisoners win suits for freedom of religion, use of lawbooks and access to other printed matter. Freedom of religion has many guises, such as demanding foods other than pork for Muslims or religious services for groups not of protestant, catholic or jewish faiths. Right to counsel pursuant to the Sixth Amendment is sought in disciplinary decisions and parole hearings. Charges of cruel and unusual punishment under the Eighth Amendment contest administrative punishments. Treatment of inmates, physical and psychological, suddenly becomes the subject of successful complaints.

CONCLUSION

Lawsuits against persons in the criminal justice system range from claims that would be brought against any citizen, to those directed at police operations, to those filed against any administrator or political subdivision. Motor vehicle accidents lead to many cases. Misuse of force is the basis for others. But the biggest expansion of litigation demands constitutional rights for people who have only recently become aware of them. Each victory encourages potential plaintiffs. Today everyone treads the path to the courtroom.

CHAPTER FOUR

REASONS FOR INCREASE IN LITIGATION

GROWING litigation against law enforcers does not necessarily signify that there are more abuses or worse injuries. This trend means that suits are popular, effective and lucrative. Some reasons for the rising tide of complaints are unique to the criminal justice system. Other explanations are common to numerous cases involving current social problems.

Since the early 1960's claims against policemen and penal workers have been increasingly filed in federal courts pursuant to the civil rights statutes. Federal trial and appellate judges are more removed from local partisanship and influence than state and local magistrates. Thus, United States courts are more apt to give an impartial hearing to charges against local officials. Appointments for life and accountability to national standards broadens the scope of the federal judiciary. A few outrageous incidents set the precedent for molding contentions of police brutality into deprivations of constitutional rights. Federal courts render judgments more expeditiously than state tribunals because of ample budgets and smaller caseloads. For these reasons grievances are framed in constitutional terms.

In the ordinary suit either plaintiff or defendant may demand a jury. Traditionally, juries have been drawn from property owners or voters. The poor or minority groups had only token representation. Counts against officials were decided by juries leaning more toward maintaining the status quo than redressing human wrongs. Broadening the base for jury selection, for example, according to racial balance of the community, gives impetus to the filing of cases.

Growing enrollments in, and founding of new law schools has released a flood of new attorneys. In the past law students began their education with a concern for social problems and justice.

However, after an expensive three years concentrated on property and financial manipulations, graduates turned to well paid practices. The emphasis in legal education has shifted from corporate-property topics to personal liberties. Law for the poor would not have been considered as a subject of study a few years ago. Today many classes delve into consumer and tenant remedies. Such interests kindle an awareness of other clashes between the disadvantaged and the law. Money has played a role in these changes. The Bar formerly defended accused indigents as a public service. Although expert talent worked on key cases, the ordinary defendant received short shrift. When tax funds began to support criminal defenses as well as prosecutions, many lawyers met persons complaining of official mistreatment. Because of their exposure to such clients, attorneys have a new consciousness of alleged oppression. A surge to rectify such wrongs has resulted.

Some years ago a judgment against a sheriff or guard was meaningless. Low pay and lack of backing from public funds made him essentially judgment proof. Now salaries have increased, and government purses are reachable. A big factor here, as elsewhere, is the prevalence of insurance. The official himself may be debt-ridden, but insurance funds substitute for his wallet.

Defenses which have protected agencies are being eroded by courts and abolished by legislatures. Sovereign immunity used to be an absolute defense for departments and political subdivisions. The theory behind this response was that the king can do no wrong. In early common law this argument prevailed because the king was divine, all knowing and all wise. It is almost ludicrous that this principle is applied to current organizations and employees. Divinity is hardly an attribute of modern government.

Sovereign immunity also clothed administrators and subordinates so long as they acted within the scope of their duty. For the officer or National Guardsman in the field this defense was almost the same as the privileges which he had for serving in a reasonable and nonnegligent manner. If he acted outside the scope of his duty, such as exercising undue force, he was liable. Commanders fared better. Few suits against them were won.

Judges developed the theory of sovereign immunity. But in many jurisdictions the principle has been viewed as so basic to litigation that it can only be removed by the legislature. Part of the rationale for this attitude is a realization by courts of the public expense that will follow such abolishment. Legislatures adopt budgets and enact tax statutes; they can appraise the cost of this move. Other judges strike down sovereign immunity as anachronistic and issue judgments on the merits of the pleadings. One compromise is to assess damages against agency or employee limited to the amount of insurance coverage. Combinations and variations of these approaches prevail throughout the country.

Judges reevaluate criminal statutes and police tactics. Many are outlawed before the man with the badge is retrained in different practices. Use of void laws and procedures can result in a verdict against the officer. Neither ignorance of the law nor good faith are adequate defenses in many jurisdictions. Thus, law enforcers are required to keep up with changes in criminal and constitutional law.

A fundamantal element in the expansion of litigation is the sprouting of dissent in America. Who better symbolizes the establishment than those sworn to uphold the law? Outcries emerge from prominent citizens and chanters in the streets. As courts uphold some claims, others are filed. Liability suits are employed to remold conduct. At least this is an orderly process; from it may come new methods of enforcement and greater respect for the law.

CONCLUSION

Many explanations exist for the surge in litigation. A particular case may be better understood if it is viewed as part of a nationwide pattern. Greater access to courts, more lawyers, expanding remedies and insurance coverage have merged at a time of protest. One result is increased lawsuits.

PART TWO...
INCIDENTS WHICH GENERATE CIVIL LIABILITY

CHAPTER FIVE

MOTOR VEHICLES

A FREQUENT claim against law enforcers arises from the vehicle accident. Exceeding speed limits or disobeying traffic signals often causes collisions. Unsafe roadblocks and crashes of pursued cars and third parties also lead to complaints. Miscellaneous other situations, such as directing traffic or commandeering vehicles, have been the bases for suits.

In many jurisdictions, statutes or ordinances relieve an officer from personal liability and shift responsibility to his employer. These provisions may give the policeman a complete or partial defense: up to a certain sum or for compensatory, but not punitive, damages. If neither judicial decisions nor specific laws waives sovereign immunity, the agency will not be liable for the acts of its officers (see governmental immunity, Ch. 4). Usually departmental insurance policies protect a policeman. However, loopholes exist, or the amount of coverage may be insufficient.

A general rule in tort cases is that the court follows the law of the place of occurrence, whether or not the trial is held there. This principle becomes important when state or local boundaries are crossed. However, the doctrine is giving way to a practice of choosing the law of the jurisdiction which has the most significant contacts with the event. For example, a collision in Massachusetts after a chase by a Rhode Island patrolman of a Rhode Island citizen probably will be viewed according to Rhode Island law. But a similar pursuit from Rhode Island to Massachusetts of a Massachusetts resident might be decided under Massachusetts law where emergency exemptions and other provisions may be different.

STATUTORY EXEMPTIONS

Most states, by statute, exempt policemen from some traffic

laws in emergencies. The Uniform Vehicle Code version reads as follows:

> § 11-106 – Authorized emergency vehicles
>
> (a) The driver of an authorized emergency vehicle, when responding to an emergency call or when in the pursuit of an actual or suspected violator of the law or when responding to but not upon returning from a fire alarm, may exercise the privileges set forth in this section, but subject to the conditions herein stated.
>
> (b) The driver of an authorized emergency vehicle may:
>
> 1. Park or stand, irrespective of the provisions of this chapter;
> 2. Proceed past a red or stop signal or stop sign, but only after slowing down as may be necessary for safe operation;
> 3. Exceed the maximum speed limits so long as he does not endanger life or property;
> 4. Disregard regulations governing direction of movement or turning in specified directions.
>
> (c) The exemptions herein granted to an authorized emergency vehicle shall apply only when such vehicle is making use of an audible signal meeting the requirements of § 12-401 (d) and visual signals meeting the requirements of § 12-218 of this act, except that an authorized emergency vehicle operated as a police vehicle need not be equipped with or display a red light visible from in front of the vehicle.
>
> (d) The foregoing provisions shall not relieve the driver of an authorized emergency vehicle from the duty to drive with due regard for the safety of all persons, nor shall such provisions protect the driver from the consequences of his reckless disregard for the safety of others.

Because of the impossibility of predicting all road and traffic conditions, a catch-all subsection is contained in (d). Never may the policeman forego his duty to drive with due regard for the safety of all persons. Other legislative restrictions are listed in the language of (a) which dictates when the privileges of (b) are exercisable. Police cars are permitted special dispensation in (c) to sound a siren and not use special lights so that unmarked vehicles will be covered. However, if flashing lights are not used in a cruiser equipped with them, courts probably will find "reckless disregard for the safety of others."

Whenever a statutory exemption is material to a decision, the outcome will depend upon whether the specific wording of the statute has been followed. Virtually all jurisdictions have enacted some form of the above-quoted section. Most legislation defines when the privileges apply as in (a), allows disregard of speed limits as in (b) 3, and contains obligations of due care as in (d). Wide variance occurs as to the remaining subsections. It cannot be overemphasized that local law must be examined.

When a policeman contends that he was acting pursuant to a statutory exemption, he must establish compliance with it. This is an affirmative defense which must be proven. One element is presence of an emergency or pursuit of a violator. Answering a fellow officer's request for help, proceeding to a fire or traveling to the scene of an accident which the policeman was required to investigate are emergency situations. Patrol cars have been denied emergency status if cruising, returning to the station or officer's home, escorting officials or clocking speeders. Depending upon the facts, following a suspicious party may be an emergency. There need not have been an actual exigency; however, the officer must have reasonably believed that it existed and show that a prudent policeman under the same conditions would have similarly responded.

A condition of using signals "capable of emitting sound audible under normal conditions from a distance of not less than five hundred feet" [Uniform Motor Vehicle Code, Section 12-401 (d), revised in 1968], is not met by a last minute sounding of a siren. Also, it may not be enough to activate the siren intermittently. The patrolman must anticipate the dangers inherent in his ignoring the rules of the road, the turning by motorists into his path, and the effect of weather and other conditions on audibility. Arbitrary exercise of privilege will not be condoned.

Under Louisiana Law, three conditions are necessary to exonerate a policeman from negligence in proceeding against an unfavorable traffic light. First, the unit must be responding to an emergency call. Second, it must have slowed down or stopped to the extent required for safe operation under the circumstances. Third, it must be utilizing at least an audible signal sufficient to alert motorists of its approach.

A deputy sheriff in Baton Rouge, Louisiana received a call from his daughter that an unidentified male followed her as she was coming home from high school. The deputy and his partner set out immediately in their unmarked cruiser. The passenger had a portable flashing light inside the vehicle and pointed it toward approaching traffic at intersections. A small siren, located under the hood, was activated by continuous depression of a button. The officers testified that the driver constantly turned the siren on and off, although the car was equipped with a manual shift. They said that they came to a complete stop before entering the intersection. Testimony from other witnesses disagreed with the officers' statements. Plaintiff was traveling at a right angle to the unmarked cruiser and was proceeding at a legal speed toward a green light in her favor. Other drivers saw the unit and stopped, but they did not hear the siren. The accident investigator characterized the sound as a muffled noise similar to that of a bumble bee in a fruit jar. The court held that the siren was neither recognizable as a warning nor loud enough to alert a prudent motorist. The officers did not fulfill the conditions necessary for the privilege of going through a red traffic light (7).

In a claim that based an officer's fault solely on his failure to continuously sound his siren, a Florida court ruled that intermittent, rather than continuous, audible warning could amount to negligence. The policeman, enroute to investigate an accident, activated the blinker light and siren to warn a vehicle that he was overtaking it. Instead of pulling over, the driver accelerated. The cruiser pursued through residential areas at over 70 m.p.h. The lights were flashing constantly, but the siren was used only at or close to intersections and when other traffic appeared. The chase neared a crossing with a heavily traveled throughway. Approximately 100 yards from the intersection, the officer observed a motorist and turned on the siren. The car on the throughway and the fleeing automobile crashed seconds later. The court acknowledged the policeman's duty to pursue and said that he was not responsible for the offender's acts. To find the officer negligent, plaintiff must show that there was a failure to use due care by not sounding continuous audible signals and that such fault caused the wreck (8).

7. *Cotton v. Transamerica Ins. Co.,* 211 So. 2d 110 (La. App. 1968).
8. *Reed v. City of Winter Park,* 253 So. 2d 475 (Fla. App. 1971).

PURSUITS

The social benefit of high speed chases is questionable. In one out of five hot pursuits someone gets killed. Half of these chases end in substantial harm. Seven out of ten result in accidents. Eighty percent of the pursuits are of minor offenders. The annual toll is 500 deaths and more than 1,000 serious injuries (9).

Many recent studies have concluded that excessive speed of emergency vehicles is unjustified because very little time is saved and so many people are endangered. Most of this research has been done in urban areas. A series of major accidents, in which speed is a proximate cause, probably will induce lawmakers to abolish the exemption. Even if it is not curtailed by legislation, courts will look at available alternatives and the seriousness of the violation, to determine whether an officer exercised due care.

When an emergency vehicle in a pursuit is defectively equipped and the signals required by statute are not in operation, fault of the operator seems clear. An Arizona court was faced with a case involving a patrol car, with brakes in poor condition, smashing into plaintiff while chasing a speeder. Testimony was conflicting as to whether the siren and flashing lights were on. For several days prior to the wreck the officer knew that the brakes had to be depressed almost to the floor before taking hold and even then would fade and grab. He had reported this to his immediate supervisor. On the night of the accident he had refused to drive the vehicle. However, he followed orders to use the cruiser. Despite the defective brakes and the presence of other motorists, the policeman pursued a traffic violator at speeds up to 65 m.p.h. To miss a motor scooter stopped in the center lane, he braked, sideswiped one auto and fishtailed into plaintiff. The policeman's negligence was the proximate cause of plaintiff's injuries (10).

PURSUIT WHEN POLICE CAR NOT IN CRASH

The issue presented in a New Jersey case was the liability of an officer for damage caused by a fleeing violator. New Jersey

9. 24 Am. Jur., Proof of Facts, Emergency Vehicle Accidents R10 (1970).
10. *City of Scottsdale v. Kokaska,* 17 Ariz. App. 120, 495 P.2d 1327 (1972).

followed the majority view that the policeman was not liable, because (1) his duty is to apprehend those whose driving makes the road dangerous to others and (2) the proximate cause of the accident was the reckless driving of the pursued, even though the chase contributed to it. The facts were that an officer observed a car parked without lights. As he approached, the lights went on and the vehicle took off at a high speed, failing to halt at a stop sign. The officer followed for about two miles with siren and lights on, and through another stop sign. Speeds accelerated to 90 and 100 m.p.h. As the fleeing auto attempted to pass a pickup, it struck plaintiff's car. The court said the policeman was not liable for the results of the offender's negligence. Police cannot be made insurers of the conduct of the culprits they chase (11).

Two Illinois officers stopped a speeder. Upon their request to see his driver's license, he was unable to produce it. During this encounter the violator was courteous and did not appear incompetent to drive. The policemen informed him that he was under arrest and ordered him to follow in his car to the station. He did so for some time and then took a sharp turn onto a side street and sped away. The unit made a U turn and gave chase. Because the siren was inoperative, the officers fired five warning shots into the air and left the dome light on. Speeds accelerated to 100 m.p.h. The driver outdistanced the cruiser on the winding, hilly road and turned off the headlights. Before the unit arrived at a through street, the violator had crashed into another car. Training officers testified that proper police techniques were to prohibit an unlicensed violator from driving; however, an ordinary traffic offender could be permitted to drive his car to the station to post bond. The jury found that the officers used due care and that the violator's conduct was the sole proximate cause of the collision. His response to the encounter with the officers did not lead them to expect him to flee while driving to the station (12).

In a complaint by a passenger in a vehicle attempting to elude policemen, a federal court in Tennessee ruled that the passenger's injury resulted from the negligence of the driver of the pursued vehicle. A fourteen year old girl was riding with her father. He was

11. *Roll v. Timberman*, 94 N.J. Super. 530, 229 A. 2d 281 (1967).
12. *Downs v. Camp*, 113 Ill. App. 2d 221, 252 N.E. 2d 46 (1969).

being followed by two officers who signaled him to stop for a minor traffic offense. The policemen told him that he might be charged with driving while intoxicated and radioed their supervisor for instructions. He sneaked back to his car and took off. The chase began. Visual and audible signals on the cruiser were activated. The motorist crossed into an intersection and hit another vehicle, killing an occupant and injuring his daughter. The officer was duty bound to pursue traffic offenders and persons fleeing arrest. It was not his fault that the violator injured others while being pursued (13).

In spite of the general rule outlined above, some recent cases have found policemen negligent when a pursued vehicle hits a third party. A typical such ruling, in New York, arose from an intersection accident. After a violator passed a stop sign without halting, an unmarked unit followed and overtook him. The car attempted to force the cruiser off the road. A three minute race continued in an urban area through sixteen red lights at speeds from 40 to 60 m.p.h. Plaintiff entered an intersection with a green light in his favor; the fleeing car was almost a block away. At no time did plaintiff hear a siren or see flashing lights. Several eyewitnesses testified that they neither heard nor saw any signals. The police said that they sounded the siren, though not constantly, and used the flashing lights on the grille. In its verdict for plaintiff, the jury apparently found that, if the siren and flashing lights had been activated, they would have warned him not to cross the intersection (14). Undoubtedly the violator was negligent, as well as the officer. But often the offender has no assets or insurance, and the only realistic target for damages will be the policeman and his department.

When a fleeing vehicle knocked a pedestrian into the air so that he landed on a person standing on the sidewalk, the latter's injuries were proximately caused by the speeding policeman's negligence in not switching on the siren. An Illinois court rejected arguments that the damages were too remote and that the siren statute was not designed to benefit persons on the sidewalk. The

13. *U. S. v. Hutchins,* 268 F.2d 69, 83 A.L.R. 2d 447 (6th Cir. 1959).
14. *Thain and Coppola v. City of New York,* 330 N.Y.S. 2d 524, 280 N.E. 2d 892 (1972).

purpose of the siren law is to warn anyone in the immediate vicinity of a danger so that he might protect himself. The decision specifically stated that an officer is negligent in not foreseeing that a pursued suspect may act in a negligent or even illegal manner to escape apprehension and thereby injure an innocent bystander (15).

If a motorist is signaled to stop and instead flees, the officer faces a dilemma. A high speed chase may result in injuries to an innocent party. Failure to pursue may encourage violators to break the law and could be dereliction of duty. Radioing for assistance is unworkable for many policemen, for example those employed by small departments. Perhaps a feasible solution would be to collect information about the driver and vehicle and obtain a summons or warrant for the owner. A statute or ordinance setting up such a procedure, based on public need for traffic enforcement and the impracticality of alternatives, probably would be upheld. To meet an owner's protest that he was not operating the car at the time, he could be allowed to defend on the grounds that the vehicle was used to violate the law without his knowledge or consent.

New devices to photograph speeders have been installed on some highways. These cameras automatically record pictures of vehicles traveling in excess of the limits. Then, citations are issued to owners at a later date.

Motor vehicle codes already contain sections which link offenses to owners. For example, parking tickets are issued to owners who must respond whether or not they were the ones who parked illegally. Forfeiture under drug laws is an action against the owner of the conveyance who may or may not have been the operator at the time. Responsibility of parents, guardians or other adults for illegal acts of minor licensees has long been accepted. Also, the owner often is liable for permitting another to use a vehicle if he is known, or should have been known, to be a negligent driver.

---

15. *Sundin v. Hughes,* 107 Ill. App. 2d 195, 246 N.E. 2d 100 (1969).

NEGLIGENT OPERATION OF EMERGENCY VEHICLE AT INTERSECTION

An officer was enroute to an emergency fire call in Louisiana. Plaintiff was stopped at a red light, and car one, opposite her across an intersection, had also halted. Car two came from a right angle, approached the crossing and slowed down to allow a taxi to turn left in front of it. The policeman arrived from behind car one, went around it, entered the intersection and collided with car two which struck plaintiff who was still stopped. All persons in these vehicles testified that they did not hear a siren nor see a flashing light before the wreck. The court said that the officer had breached his duty to fellow motorists and pedestrians when he entered the intersection without decelerating or stopping. The driver of an emergency vehicle must anticipate that, notwithstanding the use of his warning signals, others still may be proceeding through an intersection on the invitation of a green light. Noise or interference may prevent them from hearing a siren (16).

A Michigan court decided that an officer was negligent in not acting to avert a collision. The doctrine applied by the court is called *last clear chance* or *discovered peril*. It comes into play when a plaintiff, who would be barred from recovery because of contributory negligence, establishes that the proximate cause of an injury is defendant's failure to follow available evasive steps. An officer responded to a message that a vehicle had gone over an embankment. He approached an intersection with siren and flashing lights in operation. Two motorcyclists came toward the crossing at the maximum legal speed of 45 m.p.h., with a green light in their favor. The three vehicles crashed. The evidence was in conflict as to the stopping of the unit before it entered the intersection. There were jury questions as to whether the motorcyclists were in a position of helpless peril and whether the efficient cause of the accident was the officer's continuing through the intersection when the motorcyclists approached at 45 m.p.h. The officer had adequate time and distance to take preventive measures, and the verdict held him to be at fault (17).

16. *Powell v. Allstate Ins. Co.,* 233 So. 2d 38 (La. App. 1970).
17. *Jackson v. Rauch,* 18 Mich. 533, 171 N.W. 2d 551 (1969).

DEPARTMENT RULES

Violation of department regulations, which set up stricter provisions than applicable statutes, demonstrates failure to exercise due care. Even though a law permits officers to exceed speed limits, disobedience of an agency restriction is evidence of negligence. Such rules, or standard operating procedures of an organization, may be introduced in evidence as part of plaintiff's case.

An officer was using radar on a Pennsylvania four lane divided highway that had a 50 m.p.h. speed limit. A car passed his position traveling at normal speed. Moments later another vehicle went by at 70 m.p.h. The policeman immediately pulled out and accelerated to 80. His unit was unmarked and not equipped with a bubble light, but its headlights and four-way flashers were on. The siren was not sounding. As the cruiser approached the nonspeeder, the car veered slightly to the left but remained in its lane. The policeman braked hard, lost control, straddled the divider and skidded to the opposite lane into an oncoming motorist who had practically stopped to avoid the impact. Failure to activate the siren was contrary to department regulations. No explanation was given for this omission. The jury found the trooper had recklessly disregarded the safety of others. The very reason for sirens is to prevent such accidents (18).

A California court held that police bulletins on how to operate a vehicle under emergency conditions are admissible evidence. Decedent was driving through an intersection in Los Angeles on a rainy day with the green light in his favor. The windows of his automobile were closed and his radio was playing at normal volume. The squad car came through the intersection against a red light with the emergency signals flashing and siren sounding. Testimony of its speed ranged from 5 m.p.h. under to 5 to 25 m.p.h. over the posted limit of 35. The six bulletins in question stated that an officer is seldom justified in exceeding the posted limits, that few circumstances warrant greater acceleration, that when proceeding against a traffic control at a blind intersection

---

18. *Herron v. Silbaugh*, 436 Pa. 339, 260 A.2d 755 (1970).

the emergency unit should slow to approximately 15 m.p.h. and that buildings, rain and closed windows affect the audibility of a siren. An employer's safety standards demonstrate that due care requires the course of conduct outlined therein. Cross-examination of the policeman concerning his knowledge of the directives and his training in safety may aid in establishing his negligence (19).

ROADBLOCKS

The question of whether an officer exercised due care in setting up a running roadblock was answered in favor of a patrolman by a North Carolina decision. He had sued a violator, whom he attempted to halt, for personal injuries sustained in a wreck of their automobiles. A fellow officer, having pursued a stolen car for approximately 14 miles and traveling more than 100 m.p.h., radioed for assistance. The trooper entered the highway some distance ahead of the other vehicles. He decelerated from 100 m.p.h. and tried to keep in front of the stolen automobile to slow down and eventually stop it. The latter moved from one lane to the other, bumped the cruiser several times, drove onto the median, swerved into the unit and sent both vehicles off the highway. The officer was not negligent even though no statute exempted him from the requirement to give way in favor of an overtaking vehicle. The court ruled that a policeman is not deemed negligent merely because he fails to observe the Motor Vehicle Act when in pursuit of a lawbreaker (20).

In New York, an officer was told by an unidentified motorist that a black Pontiac had just backed into his parked car. To find out if a similar vehicle were involved in the incident, the policeman signaled it to halt. The car accelerated. Two other units joined in pursuit at speeds up to 100 m.p.h. through residential areas over narrow, winding and wet roads. Another patrolman, who had been contacted by radio, placed his cruiser, with the rooflight flashing, diagonally across a four lane highway in the direction the cars were heading. The obstruction was at the bottom of a rather steep hill where it could not be seen until a

19. *Dillenbeck v. Los Angeles,* 69 Cal. 2d 472, 72 Cal. Rptr. 321, 446 P. 2d 129 (1968).
20. *Collins v. Christenberry,* 6 N.C. App. 504, 170 S.E. 2d 515 (1969).

driver reached the top of the slope some 600 to 800 feet away. At the speed which the officer knew the violator to be going, the distance required to stop was 1750 feet. A taxi pulled up at the roadblock. Just then, the fleeing auto topped the hill at approximately 90 m.p.h. and crashed into the cruiser and taxi. The cab driver was thrown out and instantly killed. At trial, experts testified that setting up a roadblock which endangered anyone in the vicinity was an improper law enforcement tactic. The court stated that speeds up to 100 m.p.h. on wet and narrow roads through a residential section created an unreasonable risk to public safety and did not constitute acceptable police practices. Later information that the pursued car had been stolen did not excuse the negligence used in apprehending one known only to have been a minor traffic violator. Recklessness of the offender did not discharge the pursuers from fault (21).

PARKING

In addition to decisions that policemen have been negligent in driving their units, several cases have found them to be at fault when improperly parked. A Missouri court decided that two town marshals were liable when they parked, without dimming the lights, on the left side of a highway. They had followed an intoxicated motorist for two miles until he drove onto the shoulder. They passed his truck, turned around, came back and parked alongside it. They loaded the occupants of the truck into their unit. Then one backed the truck into a ditch, and the other guided his movements with a flashlight. Plaintiff, driving on the highway, testified that the cruiser appeared to be in the middle of the highway; he assumed that it would pass into the proper lane before they met. When the unit did not move, the cars collided. The officers alleged that they were on an emergency mission and were privileged to park anywhere. But the opinion commented on the lack of urgency of their activities, and their fault in leaving their car on the wrong side of the highway with bright lights facing oncoming traffic. They were not relieved from the exercise of due care (22).

21. *Myers v. Town of Harrison,* 438 F.2d 293 (2nd Cir. 1971).
22. *Lemonds v. Holmes,* 241 Mo. App. 463, 236 S.W. 2d 56, 22 A.L.R. 2d 418 (1951).

An Oregon decision is similar. Petitioner's vehicle ran out of gas and was pushed off the pavement on a muddy shoulder. A policeman pulled up and parked across the street to inquire why plaintiff was stopped. Approximately seven feet separated the automobiles. Lights on the squad car remained on high beam. An approaching motorist, blinded by the lights, struck petitioner's automobile. The officer was negligent in leaving his bright lights on and creating a hazard by parking so close to the disabled car (23).

A deputy sheriff apprehended a speeder in New York. They parked while he prepared a summons and discussed it with the violator and his three passengers. The unit's exact location was in dispute. Some witnesses stated that the left rear of the car was on the road, and others said that it was about two feet off the paved portion. Several persons testified that people were standing on the paved part of the highway. On the side where the cruiser stood, the shoulder was 26 feet wide, level up to 15 feet and wet but firm. Traffic at the time was exceptionally heavy. As the driver of car one approached the unit, he saw men standing alongside it and turned toward the center of the three lane road. Car two came from the opposite direction and was attempting to pass another automobile. The vehicles met head on. Plaintiff, passenger in car one, alleged that the operators of both cars and the deputy sheriff were negligent. The court agreed. The deputy sheriff did not act reasonably under the circumstances; he failed to make full use of the firm 15 foot shoulder (24).

On a January day when there was some ice and snow on the road, a trucker was traveling on a two lane highway in Kentucky. He rounded a curve and saw a squad car and a wrecker sitting side by side, blocking the road. The vehicles appeared to the trucker to be stopped, but their drivers said that they were moving slowly. As the cruiser slowly passed, the officer was directing the wrecker to assist a disabled auto. The trucker braked slightly and slid into a ditch. The distance from the curve to the obstructing automobile was estimated at from one hundred fifty to seven hundred feet. The truck speed was approximately 35 m.p.h. A dispute existed as

23. *Hornshuh v. Alldredge,* 149 Or. 419, 41 P.2d 423 (1935),
24. *Commisso v. Meeker,* 202 N.Y.S. 2d 287, 168 N.E. 2d 365 (1960).

to whether the unit's blinking lights were on. The trial judge directed a verdict for the officer and wrecker driver, but the appellate decision reversed the verdict, stating that fact issues as to their negligence should have been determined by the jury. Under these circumstances negligence could be found (25).

OFFICERS DIRECTING TRAFFIC

In an opinion that reversed a trial court dismissal of a patrolman, a New Jersey appellate court held that he could be found negligent in the following events. Two state troopers were using radar equipment. The first officer was working the radar machine 0.2 miles to the south of the point where defendant policeman acted as interceptor. The latter received a radio message to stop a white Cadillac traveling toward him. He observed two vehicles approaching in the slow lane as he stood in the fast lane and motioned for the second car, the Cadillac, to pull over. Both motorists thought that the signal was meant for car one. It stopped and was struck in the rear by car two. The driver of car two said he had no warning of an impending stop and could not move into the fast lane where the trooper stood (26).

A New Jersey policeman was directing rush hour traffic at a congested intersection where the lights were not functioning. A pedestrian was crossing when the policeman signaled a motorist to make a left turn. He had ample time to see and space to miss the pedestrian who had right-of-way on the crosswalk. The court held that the collision between the car and the pedestrian was caused by the negligence of the motorist. Even assuming that the officer was at fault in motioning the pedestrian to cross, the driver's negligence was intervening and was the proximate cause of the injuries. The policeman had a right to rely, in the absence of notice to the contrary, on the ability of motorists and pedestrians to obey the law and take care of themselves (27).

25. *Williams v. Chilton,* 427 S.W. 3d 586 (Ky. 1968).
26. *Czyzewski v. Schwartz,* 110 N.J. Super. 255, 265 A.2d 173 (1970).
27. *Gilday v. Hauchwit,* 48 N.J. 557, 226 A.2d 835 (1967).

INJURY TO PERSON ASSISTING POLICE

Under Illinois statutes a municipality is absolutely liable to a citizen who is hurt while obeying a command for assistance. A recent case was filed by a civilian employee of a city police agency. Often, at the end of his shift, he was taken home in department units. One night during such a ride, the officer-operator pursued a speeder. The policeman told plaintiff to radio headquarters and other cars for help. He continued to transmit their location throughout the chase. While traveling over a gravel road, the cruiser swerved off the street and plaintiff was seriously injured. The court ruled that the municipality was responsible, regardless of its or the officer's lack of fault (28).

DAMAGES TO COMMANDEERED PROPERTY

A Nevada court affirmed a judgment against a county for destruction of a citizen's airplane used to look for a serviceman absent without leave from the United States Coast Guard. At the request of the sheriff's office, the owner piloted the craft in the search. A statute required every man over 18 years of age to join a posse comitatus or face a misdemeanor charge. The airplane crashed and the pilot suffered memory loss. Because no one could determine the cause of the accident, the court assumed that the pilot acted with ordinary care. Nevada public policy protects a citizen following an order to assist in an arrest; therefore, the county was responsible for the pilot's loss (29).

With a rationale similar to that of the Nevada court, a Wisconsin decision held that a person, whose semi-trailers were commandeered by a trooper and parked across a highway as a roadblock, was not liable to a third party who ran into the obstruction. A deputy sheriff, chasing a traffic violator, radioed a fellow deputy to set up a roadblock. The latter directed the owner of two semi-trailers to place them across the highway. The cruiser was

28. *Meador v. City of Salem,* 51 Ill. 2d 572, 284 N.E. 2d 266 (1972).
29. *County of Clark v. Christensen,* 472 P.2d 365 (Nev. 1970).

parked on the shoulder. No flares, lights or other warning devices illuminated the hazard. The pursued vehicle plowed into the obstruction, injuring the fleeing driver. In dismissing the owner of the semi-trailers as a defendant, the court said that fault in establishing the barrier is an issue between defendant deputies and plaintiff and not pertinent to the trucker. He was obliged as a citizen to obey the officer's orders (30).

PASSENGERS

The standard of care owed to a passenger in a vehicle depends upon the relationship between the driver and the occupant. Usually, a policeman's duty toward a passenger is ordinary care under the circumstances. However, many states have enacted so-called guest statutes which limit liability only to instances of gross negligence. In several other jurisdictions case law has dictated such rules. A guest is a person who is invited to ride, chooses to do so and does not pay or confer a benefit on the owner or operator. Countless cases have construed these laws to determine the status of particular passengers. Generally, neither arrestees nor fellow officers are guests.

Gross negligence falls somewhere between inadvertance and inattention (ordinary negligence) and conscious indifference to consequences (willful, wanton and reckless conduct). Gross negligence is an extreme departure from the usual standard of care.

In a Georgia case, the duty of an officer-operator toward a prisoner passenger was to exercise ordinary care. A deputy sheriff, while carrying a prisoner, was speeding at approximately 85 m.p.h. He did not maintain a look-out ahead, and the vehicle went out of control. The arrestee was injured. He sued the deputy and the sheriff. Both were liable: the deputy for his negligent driving, and the sheriff because he directed the deputy to transport the passenger (31).

In another Georgia decision, a deputy sheriff acting on orders to accompany a fellow officer on an emergency call was not a guest.

30. *Kagel v. Brugger,* 19 Wisc. 2d 1, 119 N.W. 2d 394 (1963).
31. *Chadwick v. Stewart,* 94 Ga. App. 329, 94 S.E. 2d 502 (1956).

However, since this particular trip was an emergency mission, the applicable standard of care was to drive without reckless disregard of the safety of others. A jury question was presented as to the deputy's fault. Speeds were 80 to 100 m.p.h. on a heavily traveled highway. The unit collided with a truck traveling in the same direction which turned left to enter a private driveway. Siren and blinkers were on and the cruiser skidded 182 feet over dry pavement before the wreck (32).

A situation in which a guest was able to establish gross negligence arose in a Washington case. Defendant, an uncompensated special police officer with a guest passenger, was exceeding the limits along a city street chasing a speeder. The unit collided headon with a streetcar. No obstruction caused the swerving into the streetcar (33).

LIABILITY FOR ACTS OF SUBORDINATES

Some plaintiffs have sued superior officers for negligence of subordinates. Usually such litigation involves sheriffs or marshals and their deputies, not police supervisors and patrolmen. Future complainants probably will sue commanders and training officers under theories of inadequate instruction, failure to supervise or improper orders.

Liability of sheriffs for injuries to third persons in automobile crashes may be based on negligence of the sheriff himself. Such a finding occurred when a Georgia sheriff furnished a Ford with a Cadillac engine to a deputy who was known to be a reckless speedster. He drove 90 m.p.h. on the wrong side of the road, smashed into another car and killed its occupant. The ruling, that the sheriff's misconduct was a cause of plaintiff's damages, relied upon the sheriff's issuing the deputy a souped-up car which was difficult to control at high speeds, despite the sheriff's awareness that the deputy was a habitual speeder (34).

In order for a superior to be liable for a subordinate's acts, the latter must have been performing an official duty. Some courts

32. *Archer v. Johnson,* 90 Ga. App. 418, 83 S.E. 2d 314 (1954).
33. *Carpenter v. Thomas,* 164 Wash. 583, 3 P.2d 1001 (1931).
34. *Gay v. Healan,* 88 Ga. App. 533, 77 S.E. 2d 47 (1953).

have narrowed this requirement to such conduct as making an arrest, serving process or investigating an accident; not routine patrol or traveling to the place of an arrest. Other courts are more liberal in their construction of official acts. In a Kansas case, a sheriff was liable because of the negligence of a deputy during the scope of his employment. The deputy was responding to a radio message to investigate an accident when he plowed into an ambulance, killing one person and injuring another (35).

Some complainants have named the surety on a sheriff's bond as co-defendant. Such a surety will not be held responsible unless the sheriff is found negligent. Also, liability depends upon whether the established negligence is within the terms of the bond. The obligation relates to malfeasance, misfeasance and nonfeasance in discharge of duties. Malfeasance is wrongdoing in handling public affairs. Misfeasance amounts to doing a lawful act in an unlawful manner so as to infringe upon the rights of another. Nonfeasance means failure to perform a duty. Coverage is available when a person, toward whom the actor has an official relation, is injured. Therefore, neither hurt bystanders nor parties harmed when a deputy is not performing according to specific orders is usually within the protection of surety bonds. Responsibility under these bonds is not as broad as that of liability insurers.

Under Tennessee law a sheriff was not responsible for his deputy's negligence resulting in a vehicle collision when the deputy was routinely patroling in a county owned unit. He was on duty, but not performing any specific orders of the sheriff, when he drove across the center line into an oncoming car. Recovery against the sheriff was denied; therefore, the bondsman was not liable (36).

CONCLUSION

Automobile accidents arise from a variety of police situations. The greatest volume of this litigation comes from the employment of units as emergency vehicles. Virtually all courts allow some exemptions in the rules of the road for officers on urgent missions.

35. *Duran v. Mission Mortuary,* 174 Kan. 565, 258 P.2d 241 (1953).
36. *Waters v. McClary,* 344 F. 2d 75, 15 A.L.R. 3d 1183 (6th Cir. 1965).

However, decisions outlined in this chapter illustrate that judges and juries scrutinize the facts to determine whether privileges were abused. The general principle is due care for the safety of others, but courts delve into the totality of the circumstances to ascertain if this standard was followed.

CHAPTER SIX

FIREARMS

So many suits have been filed against officers for excessive force that the subject will be discussed in several segments of this book rather than under one heading. This chapter deals with firearms. Although some principles relating to use of guns necessarily overlap with rules pertaining to exercise of other types of force, many doctrines are unique to the most serious tool in the law enforcement arsenal.

Rules for use of deadly weapons evolved from early common law days, long before firearms existed. An officer was authorized to employ reasonable force, including deadly force, to apprehend a felon but not a misdemeanant. When these theories were formulated, the only felonies were murder, rape, manslaughter, robbery, larceny, burglary, sodomy, mayhem and arson. Danger to persons was integral to most of these crimes. Conviction meant death and forfeiture of property. Only misdemeanants were subject to lesser penalties.

In addition to capital punishment for all felonies, offenders often were mutilated or dismembered in public spectacles. Anyone facing such torture and finality was assumed to be desperate to avoid capture. He would take any means to prevent apprehension; captors needed ultimate measures to defend society from him.

Arrest for a felony was tantamount to execution. Criminal procedure was weighted heavily toward the government. Few safeguards protected suspected culprits. Prosecutions rarely ended in acquittals. Incarceration awaiting trial often, in fact, was a death sentence because of despicable jail conditions. The right to speedy hearings, exemplified in modern requirements of six months from indictment to trial, was unheard of. Rotting in prison was a reality. It was only a question of when the accused died; immediately at the hands of his apprehendors or later in the law enforcement process.

This background is important in understanding the distinction between permissible force and excessive force. The bases for doctrines of use of force can be seen as inapplicable to the present time. With drastic changes in the frequency of capital punishment, in prison facilities and in certainty of conviction, is it any wonder that principles are evolving which limit justifiable force against felons?

By modern definition, a felony is a more serious crime than a misdemeanor. The general meaning of these terms may be modified by state statutes. Usually felonies are offenses which may be punishable by imprisonment in the penitentiary for one year or more; for misdemeanors there are lesser penalties. The grade of the violation is determined by the extent of the sanction which may be inflicted and not by the actual sentence. Under prevailing codes, many misdemeanors are more dangerous to society than felonies. For example, misdemeanors such as driving while under the influence of intoxicating liquor and reckless driving result in killing thousands and maiming countless others each year. Yet, the felonies of obscene telephone calls and embezzlement, are infinitely less hazardous to public safety.

Most civil suits arising from shooting incidents have involved injuries to arrestees, to innocent bystanders during apprehensions, or to those hit by bullets discharged while an officer was mishandling a revolver. The historical discussion gives a foundation for the first category. General theories of negligence in dealing with dangerous instrumentalities govern the latter. Bystander damage is evaluated by both systems. A high degree of reasonable care and caution is required in handling guns. The hazard to anyone who may come within reach of a bullet, however unexpectedly, is foreseeable as a risk of wielding a firearm.

WHO CAN SUE

As in other types of lawsuits, cases alleging abuse of force may be filed by the hurt party or by others who have been harmed indirectly. If a person is fatally wounded, his estate or surviving heirs may initiate a complaint. Parents or guardians of a minor sue for their loss of services and future support from the infant. Spouses seek money for loss of companionship. In virtually any situation, someone has a right to claim reparation.

The estate of decedent sued an officer on the grounds that he had struck decedent over the head with a loaded revolver causing a bullet to discharge and kill him. According to the complaint, these acts were done without any provocation. The policeman moved to dismiss on the grounds that recovery under the civil rights statutes was personal and did not survive a victim's death. An Illinois court ruled that the estate could maintain the suit. Any other decision would seem inconsistent with the purpose of the law by making an officer responsible if he only injured an individual but not liable if he killed the person (37).

SELF-DEFENSE

The most basic justification for the use of firearms by an officer is self-defense, including defending the lives of others. When this answer is alleged, the courts will look behind a mere statement to ascertain whether facts substantiate it.

A deputy sheriff in Louisiana, while visiting on a Sunday afternoon, saw decedent's jeep go by. Immediately the officer went home, got his shotgun and started walking down the road to meet decedent. The deputy planned to search the jeep for illegal liquor. He hid behind a tree, stepped into the open as the vehicle approached and ordered it to halt. Decedent kept driving toward the officer and reached into the rear of the jeep. The deputy assumed such movements were made to draw a weapon which was usually carried. He opened fire when the vehicle was 75 to 90 feet from him, and he continued to shoot at close range even after the jeep had passed. These last bullets hit and killed decedent.

Twofold defenses were offered in a civil suit against the deputy, the sheriff and his surety: the deputy was afraid he would be run down, and the decedent reached for a gun to shoot him. Decedent had threatened the officer. But decedent had the reputation of a

---

37. *Davis v. Johnson*, 138 F. Supp. 572 (N.D. Ill. 1955).

braggart and had not seriously tried to carry out the threat. The trial court ruled that no hostile act was directed at the deputy; decedent was not the aggressor. The hazard from the jeep could have been avoided by stepping out of the road. Decedent was not seen with anything that appeared to be a weapon. Fatal shots were fired only after the jeep had gone by the deputy and any danger was absent. Self-defense was not accepted as an exoneration of the officer. Because he was acting in his capacity as deputy, the sheriff and the surety on his bond were also responsible (38).

A New York City policeman of 27 years experience attempted to arrest a drunken and disorderly citizen. Twice the officer was thrown to the pavement and seriously injured. He was 5 feet 8 inches tall; his attacker was 6 feet 2 and 1/2 inches tall and powerful. Bystanders were unsuccessful in giving assistance. After the policeman was in a dazed condition, he fired at his assailant and wounded an innocent third party. The latter sued and recovered because the officer was negligent in using a revolver under such conditions (39).

Early one morning in New York City plaintiff cut his stepbrother on the neck. Plaintiff's stepfather hailed two passing policemen to arrest him. After he was in custody, he was told to sit down in the living room. He got up repeatedly. The officers had seated him for the third time when he lunged at one of them. As they struggled, he struck the policeman with an empty flower pot. The other officer beat plaintiff with a nightstick. He kicked the policeman, knocked him to the floor and picked up an end table. The fallen patrolman told plaintiff to drop the table or be shot. He failed to do so and was seriously wounded in the chest. In a suit by the injured man against the officer, they were not liable. Although an end table is not usually considered a deadly weapon, an attack with it under these circumstances justified defense with a firearm (40).

WARNING SHOT

Whether or not to permit warning shots is usually a matter of

38. *Britt v. Merritt,* 45 So. 2d 902 (La. App. 1950).
39. *Wilkes v. City of N.Y.,* 127 N.Y.S. 2d 853 (1954).
40. *Woods v. City of N.Y.,* 29 A.D. 2d 550, 285 N.Y.S. 2d 149 (1967).

department policy. Even though an agency authorizes this procedure, courts will scrutinize the necessity for these shots. Too often, claims of warning shots are fabricated after the event to explain irresponsible firings.

Pursuant to a municipal ordinance, a New Jersey defendant was appointed as a reserve patrolman. The only conditions for service as a reservist were taking an oath of office and filing a bond for faithful performance of duties. Reserve officers served when needed in regular police work and at other times worked for those requesting special protection. Reserve patrolmen wore a regular uniform and badge, carried a nightstick and a .38 caliber Smith and Wesson revolver. Although defendant had been a reservist for some sixteen years, no one had ever examined his proficiency with small arms or trained him with a weapon. He was instructed that the gun could be used if his life were threatened or in a holdup. He was told that he could use force when an arrest was resisted.

On the night in question defendant had been assigned by the police chief to maintain order at a local bar and to see that the law was observed there and elsewhere in the borough. After the bar closed, a heated discussion took place outside between several young men and a trucker about a towing fee. Defendant intervened, arrested three youths and started after three others. They cursed him; one said that he would slash defendant's throat. The officer took after the fellow with nightstick in hand. The boy turned and ran across the street, ignoring an order to halt because he was under arrest. When he was 15 to 20 feet away, defendant fired at the fleeing youth's legs and wounded him in the back. Defendant said that he fired a warning shot in the boy's direction to scare him off. The jury verdict held defendant liable for both compensatory and punitive damages. Also, the municipality could be responsible on the grounds that defendant was on duty at the time of the occurrence and that he was not trained in the use of a lethal weapon before assignment to work equipped with a gun (41).

Two officers in New Jersey were informally instructed by a supervisor to pick up a seventeen year old for questioning on

41. *McAndrew v. Mularchuk,* 33 N.J. 172, 162 A. 2d 820 (1960).

suspicion, if they happened to see him. They recognized the youth at a basketball game and demanded that he identify himself. After he gave a fake name, they started to take him into custody as a parole violator. He was on parole, but they knew of no outstanding warrants or complaints against him. He suddenly pushed one of the policemen aside and bolted for the street. As the officers pursued, three warning shots were fired in the air. He ran into a 4 by 36 foot alley. One policeman yelled "halt," and then fired into the lane at a patch of light on the ground some twenty to thirty feet away. According to the officer, this was a warning shot. He was an expert marksman and a member of the police pistol team. He had aimed at the ground to avoid misfire into a house. The youth was fatally wounded by either a direct hit or ricochet.

A jury decision for defendants was reversed because of prejudice to plaintiff in the summation. In its opinion reversing the verdict, the appellate court stated that the jury must decide whether defendant shot the boy intentionally, whether death resulted from negligent firing of a warning shot or whether the warning shot hit decedent accidentally after being fired with reasonable care. Although warning shots are proper in some cases, the court said that the law imposes a duty of extraordinary care. The burden upon one who fires warning shots is almost that of an insurer. Also, the jury must decide whether the city was liable based upon the quality of training as to when to fire and upon the responsibility of an employer for acts performed by employees on duty (42).

SUSPECTS

Under common law, authority to fire at resisting or fleeing felons did not include shooting at suspects. The justification covered only circumstances in which a felony had happened. Firing at a person whom the officer reasonably believes has committed or is attempting to commit the crime is unwarranted unless a felony has been perpetrated. The policeman shoots at his

42. *Wimberly v. Paterson,* 75 N.J. Super. 584, 183 A. 2d 691 (1962).

peril. If he injures someone assumed to be a felon and no such crime has occurred, the officer is civilly responsible.

Between midnight and 1:00 a.m., plaintiff, a high school senior in North Carolina, was walking home with three or four companions. They were overtaken by a car filled with white youths who taunted them and sped past. The vehicle returned. One passenger threw a tire tool at the boys. Plaintiff retrieved the metal bar. After several others joined the fracas, the auto scurried away. In response to a radio call to another unit, defendant officer and his partner arrived on the scene. The boys scattered. Plaintiff, who was the last to flee, had the tire tool in his hand. Defendant claimed that the object looked like a gun, but his partner saw neither gun nor tool. The cruiser pursued plaintiff. For six blocks he outran it until the unit trapped him in a narrow lane. Headlamps and a streetlight illuminated him with the tool in his hand. The youth ran out of the alley past the cruiser. Defendant got out of the unit, drew and cocked his pistol and chased the boy for about sixty feet. Defendant called for him to stop; plaintiff did so, dropped the tool and turned to face defendant. In lowering his revolver, defendant said that he accidentally pulled the trigger and hit the teenager in the thigh.

Plaintiff charged that the shooting was deliberate, that the officer took aim again and only lowered the barrel when his partner appeared. The boy was loaded in the cruiser and taken to the police station (contrary to department procedures) for advice on what to do with the bleeding youth. The trial court awarded out-of-pocket damages of $448.00 to plaintiff. But the appellate court held the amount inadequate and remanded the case to the trial court for additional damages to cover all consequences of the wound, including pain and suffering, and for consideration of whether punitive damages were appropriate (43).

An adolescent plaintiff and companions in Pennsylvania saw a squad car stop near them. Because of their fear of being picked up on suspicion, they left the area. They proceeded toward plaintiff's home and paused in a back yard to see if they were being followed. Defendant officer was pursuing them. When they

43. *Jenkins v. Averett,* 424 F. 2d 1228 (4th Cir. 1970).

stopped, he shot plaintiff in the leg. Defendant kicked the boy while he was down and told him to "shut up" when he inquired why he had been wounded. The youth was taken in the cruiser to a hospital but was refused permission to telephone his parents or to have a friend accompany him. Defendant moved to dismiss a complaint under the federal civil rights act. The court denied the motion; if the contentions are proven, plaintiff is entitled to recover against defendant (44).

MISDEMEANANTS

A policeman in New Jersey was patroling on his motorcycle when he observed a man and a teenage girl on the sidewalk. The girl appeared afraid and was backing up as he advanced toward her. The officer approached and asked the fellow to talk with him. As the man walked away, the policeman grabbed him, but he wrenched loose and ran. The officer chased him and shouted for him to stop. Since he was getting away, the patrolman commanded the fellow to stop or be shot. He kept running and four rounds were fired at the ground. As he continued, the fifth bullet, aimed at his legs, missed. The sixth cartridge, from a distance of at least 100 feet, hit him. The most serious offense for which he could have been arrested was violation of the disorderly persons act: a misdemeanor. The court held that the shooting constituted an atrocious assault and battery. There was no evidence of self-defense. The policeman had no right to shoot the fleeing man even though there was no other way of preventing his escape (45).

Plaintiff claims that he was standing on a public sidewalk in front of a public cafe when defendant officer, without provocation or legal cause, shot him in the stomach and immediately departed without rendering aid to him. Defendant's version of the incident is that he shot plaintiff while he resisted lawful arrest for disturbing the peace. Plaintiff pled guilty to the charge. In denying the officer's motion to dismiss the civil rights complaint, the

44. *Roberts v. Trapnell,* 213 F. Supp. 49 (E.D. Pa. 1962).
45. *Noback v. Town of Montclair,* 33 N.J. Super. 420, 110 A.2d 339 (1954).

Mississippi court stated that the guilty plea would not bar this civil action. Even if plaintiff were disturbing the peace, defendant was not authorized to shoot him (46).

Two men in New Mexico were involved in an argument about a fender bender when one of them summoned a policeman who was driving by. The other fellow started fighting with the officer, cutting his face and knocking him against the car. The first man intervened, and the policeman's assailant walked away some 15 to 20 feet. The officer called out that the assaulter was under arrest. After drawing his revolver, the trooper fired at the attacker. The court held the policeman liable for using more force than necessary to arrest a misdemeanant. Either the shooting was an attempt to apprehend the assaulter or was in blind rage; there was no justification whichever was the reason (47).

FELONS

Cases in the past two sections have involved shootings of suspects and misdemeanants. Officers have no right to fire at such persons except in self-defense. Although shooting at a felon has been treated differently historically, recent cases demonstrate that firing at fleeing felons is not always permitted.

Two New Orleans, Louisiana officers were investigating a complaint when a Mustang recklessly sped past them. They jumped into their cruiser and pursued it. The flashing lights and siren were activated, but the Mustang with four young men inside continued speeding through the city. Although the passenger officer fired four shots at the Mustang, the chase went on until the driver lost control and crashed into a parked car. The unit pulled up and the troopers emerged with guns in their hands. Three of the juveniles surrendered promptly, but the driver fled. One policeman ran after him, fired and killed him.

The officers contended that they had probable cause to arrest the boys for theft: a felony. The court agreed because of the continued flight when the youths knew the police were pursuing and the pattern of such behavior by car thieves in the city. Also,

46. *Jackson v. Martin,* 261 F. Supp. 902 (N.D. Miss. 1966).
47. *Padilla v. Chavez,* 62 N.M. 170, 306 P.2d 1094 (1957).

the officers reasonably believed that the decedent could not be immediately apprehended without the use of deadly force. In answering the question of whether the policeman who shot decedent was liable, the court discussed Louisiana statutes which limit deadly force to situations involving great bodily harm or danger to life. Car theft is a felony relating only to property. Louisiana extended the common law that deadly force cannot be employed to arrest a misdemeanant to include felons not causing peril to life or personal safety. Decedent was killed to prevent his escape. If captured and convicted of both auto theft and resisting arrest, his punishment would not have exceeded a few years of imprisonment. The officer who did not shoot decedent is not liable; the one who did is responsible (48).

In denying preliminary motions, a Delaware court held that a jury must decide whether or not excessive force was used in the following situation. Two troopers were on routine patrol when they observed a speeder. They signaled him to stop. He accelerated, and a chase was underway. Speeds ranged to 120 m.p.h. The offender's car, when the cruiser was alongside it, swerved as if to ram the unit. No collision occurred. The violator lost control soon afterwards and struck a stone wall and a tree. He jumped from the wreck and ran. The officers chased on foot, yelled that they were policemen and ordered him to stop or they would shoot. A bullet was fired at the offender's feet. He kept running. The officer, about 125 to 175 feet from him, shot and killed him. The troopers contended that a felony had been committed in the attempt to ram their unit. In trying to arrest for this felony, they claimed authority to use deadly force. Plaintiff argued that they had no reasonable grounds to believe that decedent's jerking the wheel of the vehicle was an assault with intent to murder rather than a swerving to control a car at high speed. The court ruled that proper inferences from the facts must be resolved by a jury (49).

A Hartford, Connecticut officer was sitting in his parked cruiser when a new Pontiac went by. The car accelerated as it passed the marked unit. In the pursuit that followed, the Pontiac outdistanced the policeman and soon was located with one wheel on

48. *Sauls v. Hutto*, 304 F. Supp. 124 (E. D. La. 1969).
49. *West v. Wheatley*, 313 F. Supp. 656 (D. Del. 1970).

the sidewalk, lights on and unoccupied. Upon looking around, the officer saw decedent coming out of an alley. He turned and ran into the back yard of a house. The officer ordered him to stop. Decedent yelled out a dèfiant statement and began to disappear over a fence. The trooper fired and killed him. The court ruled that decedent was shot in an attempt to resist arrest for the felony of stealing the Pontiac. The officer had reasonable grounds for believing that decedent had committed this felony; no more than necessary force was used to effect the apprehension (50).

Following a burglary of a National Guard armory in New Mexico, an officer discovered four stolen rifles in a ditch beside a country road. A deputy sheriff and an F.B.I. agent hid in a cotton field about eighty feet from the ditch hoping to apprehend whoever came to retrieve the weapons. After dark a car approached and parked near the rifles. Its lights were turned off. A man got out, grabbed the guns and hurried back toward the automobile. The officers jumped up, identified themselves and called for him to halt. The fellow continued toward the vehicle until the agent fired a shot; the rifles were dropped. The motor of the car started, and it began moving away with its lights on. The deputy fired his sawed-off shotgun twice at the vehicle to blow out the tires. The buckshot struck the upper portion of the automobile, killing the operator. The judge held that the deputy was justified in shooting at the vehicle to prevent the driver's escape. The officer had an obligation to stop the felon. He should not be liable for performing his duty (51).

THIRD PARTY INJURED

Although courts will scrutinize incidents in which a third party is wounded while an officer is making an arrest, there are defenses available to the policeman. Whether he is liable depends upon his use of due care. However, negligence of the injured person may absolve the policeman.

In Virginia, three officers were out in the early morning hours to catch a person wanted for several felonies. Because the criminal

50. *Martyn v. Donlin,* 151 Conn. 402, 198 A. 2d 700 (1964).
51. *Alaniz v. Funk,* 69 N.M. 164, 364 P. 2d 1033 (1961).

had a long record, he was expected to be armed and to resist arrest. The troopers agreed that one of them would go to the rear of a house, where the felon was spending the night, and the other two would knock at the front door. They anticipated that he would try to escape by the back door. When he emerged from the back with gun in hand, the officer called for him to halt. He shouldered a weapon. The policeman fired but missed and ran after the felon. Upon seeing a man on the sidewalk in front of the house, the trooper shot again without calling out a warning. The bullet struck a fellow officer who was wearing civilian clothes and had left his station on the front porch to aid in the apprehension.

The wounded officer sued the trooper. In holding no liability, the court relied upon the doctrines of sudden emergency and assumption of the risk. Defendant was acting under the stress of an emergency when the armed felon attempted to escape. His actions are judged with a different measure from that used in weighing acts done under normal conditions. Plaintiff left the comparative safety of the front porch and voluntarily exposed himself to the hazard of gunfire from defendant in the dark foggy night. Plaintiff assumed the risk of the injury incurred; therefore, defendant is relieved of legal responsibility even though he may be negligent (52).

A New York City policeman interrupted a holdup in the back room of a store. The bandits fired at him. He returned the shots when he was about 8 feet from them. One bullet was aimed at the first felon and four at the other. A hostage alongside the latter was hit by the four rounds. The city was liable for the officer's negligence on the theory that he had not received sufficient and proper instruction in when to fire a revolver. The decision was affirmed on appeal even though there was no proof of any prescribed, accepted or recognized training of members of municipal agencies in using small arms in emergencies (53).

A New Jersey mounted patrolman was assigned to keep traffic moving in the busiest section of central downtown. He went into a store to locate the owner of an illegally parked vehicle. Inside, the manager was arguing with a man holding a shopping bag. The

---

52. *Berry v. Hamman,* 203 Va. 596, 125 S.E. 2d 851 (1962).

53. *Meistinsky v. N.Y.,* 285 App. Div. 1153, 140 N.Y.S. 2d 212 (1955); aff'd 132 N.E. 2d 900 (1956).

manager called to the officer that the man had stolen the contents of the sack. As the trooper attempted to arrest him, he shoved the officer aside, dropped the bag and fled into the street knocking down a woman in his path. When the patrolman reached the sidewalk, he called four times for the man to halt. The flight continued, and the officer shot at the fellow's legs to stop him. Before firing, the policeman looked to see if anyone were in the direct line of his aim. He knew that pedestrians would be nearby but he did not look elsewhere. Although no one was in the line of fire, the bullet deflected off the street and struck a girl on the sidewalk.

In a suit by the girl, the jury resolved that defendant officer was not responsible. However, a new trial was ordered because of error in instructions to the jury. The goods which the man was unlawfully taking were valued at $36.87; New Jersey statutes make this a high misdemeanor. In New Jersey the common law distinction, in permissible force between felonies and misdemeanors, has been modified to apply between high misdemeanors and petty crimes. Despite defendant's authorization to shoot at the fleeing man, liability could result from not exercising reasonable prudence to avoid injuring innocent persons. The jury must consider this theory in a new trial (54).

SHOOTING FROM MOVING VEHICLE

If there is a dispute about what happened, the jury must decide which facts to believe. Testimony is often in conflict in cases resulting from injuries sustained when officers have fired from moving vehicles. The extreme hazard to the public from such shooting is obvious. This plus the severity of the situation and the necessity for using a gun will be carefully evaluated. Inferences from the evidence and the credibility of witnesses are weighed by the jury.

Two officers in Mississippi observed plaintiff at about 3:00 a.m. speeding in the city, almost overturning his car as he went in and out of an alley and running a motorist off the road. They had

54. *Davis v. Hellwig,* 21 N.J. 412, 122 A. 2d 497, 60 A.L.R. 2d 866 (1956).

arrested plaintiff for drunkenness ten days earlier and were aware that he was endangering his own safety and that of others. They pursued with flashing lights and siren blaring. He ignored their signals, and his car began weaving from one lane to the other. In order to halt him, they shot at the rear tires. Bullets punctured the tires, causing him to lose control and suffer bruises on his head as the car stopped.

Plaintiff sued the policemen for personal injuries and property damage. Plaintiff testified that he was driving cautiously and at a lawful speed when he was fired upon without warning and with no knowledge that the pursuers were officers. The jury apparently did not accept plaintiff's version of the events and rendered a verdict for defendants. The appellate court affirmed the verdict. The opinion stressed that if the jury had believed that the officers were firing at plaintiff or his car generally and a bullet had struck the vehicle, glanced and hit plaintiff, the defendants would have been liable for both personal injuries and property damage. However, the jury had decided that the shots were aimed at the rear tires without any intention of harming either plaintiff or his automobile. The firing was to stop the car and lawfully arrest plaintiff; therefore, defendants were not negligent (55).

Three men were driving home on a highway in Tennessee when they saw an automobile overtaking them and someone in the car waving a flashlight. Assuming that the person might be trying to hold them up, they accelerated. After a mile or two, they observed a figure lean out of the pursuing vehicle and shoot at them. The bullets went into the car and punctured the left rear tire, causing the vehicle to overturn and hurt all of the occupants. The driver died from his injuries. The shots were fired by a constable who alleged that he was attempting to arrest the parties for public drunkenness and driving while drunk. The operator had consumed one beer; the passengers each had had two beers. They said that they were not intoxicated. They were acquitted of the misdemeanor of public drunkenness.

The trial court directed a verdict for defendants: the constable and his bondsman. On appeal, the verdict was reversed on the

55. *State for Use of Holmes v. Pope,* 54 So. 2d 658 (Miss. 1951).

grounds that the jury should have decided whether defendants were liable. The appellate court stated that an officer has no right to shoot at one guilty of only a misdemeanor to stop his flight or prevent escape. Allowing him to flee is better than taking his life or doing him great bodily harm. Even though the bullets were aimed at the tires, the shooting was so hazardous to human life as not to be tolerated. The jury could have found that the firing was calculated to produce and did cause death to the driver and severe injuries to the passengers. The bondsman also could be held responsible because the acts were done by the constable while performing his job (56).

A Nebraska sheriff served plaintiff with a summons for willful reckless driving. Shortly afterwards the sheriff observed plaintiff speeding and pursued at a rate in excess of 100 m.p.h. but was unable to overtake him. After chasing for about three miles, the sheriff radioed his deputies to set up a roadblock. The deputies parked their cruisers across the highway with flashing lights on. When the deputies saw plaintiff's automobile approaching, they went onto the highway and waved their arms to signal him to stop. One of them was armed with a Thompson .45 caliber submachine gun, and the other had a revolver. Instead of halting, plaintiff's vehicle turned away from the barrier. The deputy with the submachine gun discharged a warning burst across the path of the car and shot at the tires. The other deputy fired at the right front tire. Plaintiff's speed was estimated at around 90 m.p.h. as he passed the deputies. Three bullets struck the right side of the vehicle; one cartridge penetrated the right front tire causing it to deflate. The automobile stopped 250 yards away.

Plaintiff sued the sheriff and deputies. The verdict was for defendants. Plaintiff appealed, and the jury decision was affirmed. The appellate court held that whether the defendants used excessive force was a jury question. The court stressed that 1) plaintiff was a misdemeanant, 2) although no one was hurt, the shooting affected the safety of all persons upon the highway and 3) the use of firearms to stop a vehicle is an extreme measure which should be employed in only the most serious cases.

56. *State ex rel. Harbin v. Dunn,* 282 S.W. 2d 203 (Tenn. 1943).

Apparently the jury considered all of these matters; therefore, their verdict was not reversed (57).

MISHANDLING FIREARMS

In addition to suits based upon improper shooting, several cases have dealt with injuries resulting from mishandling of weapons. An extremely high standard of care is demanded in manipulating a lethal instrument.

A probationary patrolman, who was undergoing a mandatory training course with the City of New York, was cleaning his police revolver at home when it fired and injured his wife. He had completed five of sixteen sessions on firearms and was cleaning the gun preparatory to an inspection the following day. Because an officer is required to carry his weapon at all times and to respond to call anytime, he was acting within the scope of his employment when he cleaned the revolver at home. Both the officer and the city were liable to the wife. The policeman mishandled the weapon. Responsibility of the city was predicated upon inadequate training of the officer and negligence of an employee while performing his duty (58).

An officer in New Jersey was on a day off at his apartment. He went into the bathroom and, as required by department rules that he carry his revolver at all times when off duty, he was wearing an off duty holster with a loaded weapon inside. The holster attached to his belt was his personal property; the revolver belonged to the department. He removed the gun from the holster with his right hand, intending to place it on the water tank about three feet from him. When the revolver was about one foot away from his body, it discharged. On the other side of a common wall, a youngster taking a bath was severely wounded.

The officer stated that the gun had fallen out twice before when he went to the bathroom, and that it was necessary for him to remove the revolver from the holster in order to drop his trousers. Experts testified that the gun would not have fired unless he had pulled the trigger. He said that he did not know why the weapon

57. *Breese v. Newman,* 179 Neb. 878, 140 N.W. 2d 805 (1966).
58. *Hacker v. City of N. Y.,* 46 Misc. 2d 1003, 261 N.Y.S. 2d 751 (1965).

discharged; he did not drop it, strike anything with it or pull the trigger. The jury found him liable and also the City of Newark. He was at fault in mishandling the gun. The basis for the city's responsibility was active wrongdoing through inadequate training in safe use of the revolver. There was no instruction in off duty handling and no retraining program. The officer had not fired his gun since his appointment, a period of sixteen and one-half months. The recruit school instruction was characterized as far below standard; inservice training was nonexistent. The department had no specifications for off duty holsters although it required officers to have these holsters and to carry the issued revolver (59).

NATIONAL GUARD

Liability of a National Guardsman for excessive use of force is determined by state and federal civilian courts. Standards for the guardsman's activities may depend upon whether the National Guard has been federalized and is under the command of the President of the United States or whether it is called out by a state governor and is under his control. In any event, recruitment, equipment and training are paid for and designed on the federal level.

Under prevailing law a guardsman generally is not liable when he follows an order without malice unless it is obviously illegal. Soldiers are expected to obey unquestioningly and not form a debating team at each command. Case law is unclear as to whether the rules of use of force pertaining to policemen also define the standards of guardsmen. Even though the rules may be identical, most actual situations involving guardsmen are emergencies. Some flexibility is permitted due to the urgent nature of affairs. In the past decade or so, the National Guard has used arms in quelling civil disturbances. A majority of the states have enacted so-called riot statutes which expand authorization of force for all officers. Local provisions must be examined to ascertain the limitations of these statutes.

---

59. *Peer v. Newark,* 71 N.J. Super. 12, 176 A. 2d 249 (1961).

One of the biggest problems in a suit against a guardsman is identifying the defendant. Few plaintiffs know who among a line of soldiers wounded them. Usually guardsmen will be acting in concert and not performing alone. Complainants have sued superiors on theories of improper orders or inadequate training. Courts rarely will engage in Monday morning quarterbacking of officers who faced angry crowds, rock hurlers or snipers. Training is mandated by federal law and can hardly be ruled inadequate as to any particular local commander.

OFF DUTY

Employers often are held responsible for acts of employees in the course of employment. Whether a policeman is on duty is a more difficult question than whether ordinary employees are acting within the scope of their jobs, because officers usually are expected to perform police work 24 hours every day. However, the following case shows one example of an officer who clearly was not on duty.

The question posed in a New Jersey lawsuit was: is the city liable for injuries sustained by a participant in an illegal dice game who was shot with a police firearm by a drunken officer who extorted the proceeds of the gambling? The court answered no. Plaintiff contended that the city was responsible. An ordinance required officers to be always on duty, and the city had entrusted him with a weapon. The court replied that the policeman had abandoned his duty. He was acting in furtherance of his own interests and not for the benefit of the city, even though he showed his badge to the gamblers before demanding the money. No allegation was made that the city had knowledge that he would commit such acts. No negligence of the city was proven (60).

LIABILITY OF INSURERS

Insurance policies often cover the negligence of policemen. The terms of each contract must be examined to discover if coverage

60. *Snell v. Murray,* 117 N.J. Super. 268, 284 A. 2d 381 (1971).

exists. A company may defend by answering that the improper acts were performed while the employee was not on the job. An employer's insurer attempted to avoid payment on another theory in the following situation.

In the process of making an illegal arrest, a deputy town marshal of Louisiana shot plaintiff. Based on a finding that the shooting was intentional, the trial court held the employer's insurer not responsible. The issue on appeal was whether the policy covered a deliberate act. It is an elementary principle of public policy that no one can insure against his own intentional acts. However, the fact that acts of an employee are deliberate does not confer that characterization on the employer. Coverage is viewed from the position of the party insured (the employer) and from this vantage point the employee's shooting was accidental and within the policy (61).

DEPARTMENT RULES

The general rules for firing weapons set up a distinction between felonies and misdemeanors. Department regulations may be different from such principles. Violation of department standards is evidence of negligence. A law enforcer is expected to know and follow his employer's guidelines.

At 12:15 a.m. two plainclothes officers in an unmarked unit observed a 55 year old man driving in a high crime area of Los Angeles, California. They decided to stop him for questioning. They pulled up alongside his car. The passenger raised his badge, shined a flashlight on it and shouted for the motorist to pull over for the police. He was slightly hard of hearing and kept on driving. They continued next to him, again showed a badge and honked the horn. He made several turns with the officers pursuing. When he reached under the seat, they became alarmed although he did not exhibit a weapon.

Two other plainclothesmen in another unmarked cruiser heard a broadcast about the chase. They parked partially across an intersection ahead of the cars, and one of them waved a red light

61. *Balthazar v. Williams,* 254 So. 2d 470 (La. App. 1971).

to alert oncoming traffic. An officer alighted from the vehicle with a double-barreled shotgun. When the motorist's car stopped at a traffic light, the officer tapped with a muzzle on the closed left front window of the automobile. The fellow appeared to be frozen at the wheel so the policeman lifted the gun, leaned forward and displayed his badge. Thereupon, the vehicle accelerated. The officers testified that the car knocked the policeman with the gun backwards and headed toward the other officer. The one with the shotgun fired through the left rear window and his partner aimed four revolver rounds into the left front window. The man was killed instantly. At the time of the shooting several marked units were converging on the street from two directions. Decedent had committed no crime. His wallet was found under the front seat where he had apparently placed it during the pursuit. A motorist who was in the lane next to the man testified that the car had not accelerated before the shot was fired. Other witnesses corroborated this testimony.

After a verdict for defendants at trial, the appellate court reversed because the trial judge erroneously decided that the theory of negligence was not applicable and the police manual was not admissible evidence. Negligence of the officers could be based on a finding that they acted unreasonably against a person who believed that he was about to be robbed. There were fact questions as to whether the vehicle moved before the shooting, and even if it did, the necessity of firing is questionable. Also, negligence could arise from the plainclothesmen's not permitting available uniformed officers in marked units to stop the man. Whether fault was shown in using a muzzle to tap on the window should have been considered by the jury. The police tactical manual pertaining to the use of firearms was erroneously withheld from the jury's evaluation. In circumstances such as this case, the regulations authorized deadly force only if necessary to save an officer, a citizen, a brother officer, or a prisoner from death or grave bodily harm (62).

A nineteen year old had stolen a dune buggy and was chased at night by a policeman in downtown Miami, Florida. The youth

62. *Grundt v. Los Angeles,* 2 Cal. 3d 575, 86 Cal. Rptr. 465, 468 P.2d 825 (1970).

abruptly turned into a brightly lit parking lot and crashed into a wall at the end of the lot. The cruiser missed the turn and skidded to a stop on the street. The officer ran to the wrecked dune buggy. Two other policemen joined the pursuit on foot. By then the boy was scaling a chain link fence topped with barbed wire. The first officer stopped some thirty-five feet from the fence and fired a fatal shot. The other two policemen were closer than 35 feet to the decedent when the revolver went off. The court found that they could have apprehended the decedent without deadly force; neither of them had drawn their weapons. Numerous other troopers were in the vicinity at the time of the shooting. Decedent could have been captured by such officers if he had escaped the three behind him.

Department rules specifically prohibited discharge of guns to capture the driver of a stolen vehicle unless in self-defense or unless the theft was incidental to the commission of another felony. When decedent was shot, both of his hands were on the fence, he was unarmed and he had displayed no article which reasonably could have been mistaken for a weapon. No self-defense evidence was established. Department rules also stipulated that an officer should never pull the trigger if there was any doubt of the justification for firing. The court stated that the officer did not follow agency regulations. Because the policeman was acting within the scope of his employment, both the individual and the department were liable to decedent's parents for the intentionally inflicted death (63).

CONCLUSION

The essential principle which surfaces from an examination of the law pertaining to firearms is that extreme care is necessary. Courts are wary of claims of cautious warning shots going astray. Early cases held that capturing an escaping felon was of paramount importance to society. These rules are eroding. Modern judges speak of the value of human life and the ultrahazardous nature of guns. Self-defense is always acceptable as an answer to

63. *Mayhall v. City of Miami,* U.S.D.C.S.D. Fla. #71-775-Civ. J.L.K. (1970).

wounded persons. But the circumstances must justify reasonable belief that the life of the officer, or of another, was endangered. Inadequate firearms training is increasingly alleged by complainants. Departments and individual officers are liable for negligence in wielding guns unless necessity for shooting is clearly apparent.

CHAPTER SEVEN

ASSAULT AND BATTERY

ASSAULT and battery in civil law are intentional torts. Most of the cases in Chapter Five (Motor Vehicles) are grounded on negligence. The lawsuits discussed in Chapter Six (Firearms) contain a mixed group of intentional and negligent acts. Liability for negligence arises from a foreseeable injury. The intent required in assault and battery is not necessarily a desire to cause harm; it is based on the doing of a voluntary act which to a substantial certainty will injure another. By the doctrine of transferred intent, the purpose of hurting one individual is transferred to the person actually damaged. For example, if X draws back his fist to hit Y and instead strikes Z, X has battered Z.

Assault and battery are not the same. Both are not applicable to all cases. Assault is committed when an individual is caused to dread a harmful or offensive contact. No actual touching is necessary; assault is a movement that alerts one to a threat which the attacker has the apparent ability and opportunity to immediately carry out. Mere words, however violent, do not constitute an assault. A threat which obviously cannot be translated into reality is not an assault. Battery is an unpermitted contact by an individual directly or by means of a force which he has activated. The person who is battered need not have been aware of the contact before it occurred or when it took place. For example, an unconscious drunk, who is beaten with a nightstick, has been battered. If he is awake and realizes that the blow is coming, he has been assaulted and battered.

The terms assault and battery frequently are linked whether or not both apply. Generally both assault and battery are present though they occur at different points in time and need not both take place in any particular situation.

Some contacts between individuals are inevitable in a crowded world. Such physical contacts as jostling on the street or in a packed bus are accepted as part of the movement in society. Other touching is consented to in sports or surgery.

Law enforcers are permitted to exert reasonable force in making a legal arrest. When they exceed this limit, the privilege no longer exists, and they become assaulters and batterers. In most jurisdictions a victim of an illegal apprehension is allowed to protest with reasonable force. This rule has been modified by statutes in some states so that arrestees must submit and challenge the legality later. But no one is bound to passively endure abuse; reasonable resistance is always allowable.

SELF-DEFENSE IN A LEGAL ARREST

Plaintiff spent several hours in a bar in North Dakota drinking and visiting. By midnight he was intoxicated and sobbing loudly. His wife and the proprietor took plaintiff's arm to help him leave, but he resisted. Defendant deputy sheriff, who was drinking in the bar but not intoxicated, assisted the owner. Each took one of plaintiff's arms to lead him outside. Defendant told plaintiff's wife that he would take plaintiff for a walk. Defendant and another person guided plaintiff across a vacant lot. He insisted on returning to the bar, although defendant was trying to get him to go home. When plaintiff became more uncooperative, defendant said that he would arrest plaintiff for intoxication in a public place unless he went home. Others joined in attempting to convince him to leave. He adamantly refused and deliberately kicked defendant in the crotch. As the deputy doubled up with pain, he was booted in the shoulder. Defendant partially straightened up and struck plaintiff in the face, breaking the left lens of his glasses and seriously injuring his eye.

Plaintiff sued defendant, the sheriff and his surety for loss of his eye. Judgment was for defendants. The deputy, in making a legal arrest, was not only not obliged to retreat but rather had a duty to overcome resistance. There is no evidence that defendant intended to hit plaintiff in the eye; he lashed out in self-defense. The force used must be measured by the circumstances of the blow, not by the incidental results. The presumption, that an officer performs his duty correctly and acts with ordinary caution and in good faith, prevails unless overcome by definite evidence to the contrary; no such proof was offered (64).

After a Louisiana deputy sheriff received a radio report regarding a suspected drunken driver, he observed a vehicle matching the description given on the broadcast. He stopped the automobile as two other units drove up. Plaintiff driver stepped out of the car. Defendant deputy told plaintiff that he was under arrest for driving while intoxicated. Plaintiff reacted belligerently and, while arguing with the deputy, reached into the side pocket of his trousers. Defendant pulled a nightstick from his belt and struck plaintiff a severe blow on the side of the head. Plaintiff was about 5 feet 7 inches tall and weighed approximately 150 pounds. Defendant was over six feet and weighed about 250. However, defendant alleged self-defense because he believed plaintiff was reaching for a weapon. The court held that the deputy had reasonable grounds to fear bodily harm when plaintiff reached into his pocket; defendant's striking him with a nightstick was justified (65).

SUBDUING ARRESTEE

In the small hours of the morning three officers were cruising near the business section of Salt Lake City, Utah. They noticed an automobile parked close to a service station under construction and near a shed containing tools and equipment. Although the car lights were off, the engine was running. They left but returned shortly. The vehicle was still there so they pulled up beside it to interrogate plaintiff, the occupant. One trooper asked plaintiff for his driver's license. He exhibited a temporary permit which listed no personal information except name and address. Additional identification was requested. He refused to display an army identification card which the policeman observed as plaintiff thumbed through the papers in his wallet. When asked what he was doing in that neighborhood, he replied that it was none of the officer's business. The trooper searched plaintiff and put him into

64. *Schell v. Collis,* 83 N.W. 2d 422 (N.D. 1957).
65. *Crawford v. Maryland Cas. Co.,* 169 So. 2d 612 (La. 1964).

the cruiser, telling him that he was either going to identify himself and produce the vehicle registration or be taken to jail. Plaintiff did not comply and tried to leave. A struggle ensued. Plaintiff hit one policeman with the handcuffs before being subdued by a blow on the head with a flashlight. He was taken to jail and charged with vagrancy, assault and battery and resisting an officer.

All criminal trials were terminated in favor of plaintiff. He then sued the three policemen for assault, battery, false arrest and malicious prosecution. Defendants prevailed on all counts. The court held that plaintiff had been legally arrested when the scuffle occurred; the force employed to detain plaintiff was reasonable. Not guilty verdicts at trial show that the government was unable to prove the charges beyond a reasonable doubt; this is not equivalent to a finding that the arrest was illegal. The prosecutor independently determined that probable cause existed before the criminal complaints were signed by the policeman. Therefore, the complaint of malicious prosecution was unfounded (66).

Plaintiff was arrested for driving while intoxicated by an Illinois officer. While apprehending plaintiff, the policeman struck him so violently that he lost the sight of one eye. A jury found the officer and his employer liable to plaintiff. The employer's fault was premised on negligence in hiring the patrolman. He had been put to work on a 30 day trial basis without any training. No one had examined his background before employment. If they had checked, they would have discovered that he had been involved in many street brawls and convicted of grand larceny (67).

Late at night plaintiff crashed into the back fender of a car in East Chicago Heights, Illinois. He talked with the owner, who knew him, and went home. The owner reported the damage to two officers parked three blocks away and took them to plaintiff's home. They aroused plaintiff, discussed the accident and left with the owner to file a complaint. After doing so, they returned to arrest plaintiff. He resisted and repeatedly inquired about being hauled to jail. They refused to answer questions and insisted that plaintiff accompany them even before he could put on his shoes. In taking him from the house to the unit, they scuffled from the

66. *Wendelboe v. Jacobson,* 10 Utah 2d 344, 353 P. 2d 178 (1960).
67. *Peters v. Bellinger,* 22 Ill. App. 2d 105, 159 N.E. 2d 529 (1959).

front porch to the yard. Plaintiff was beaten with a nightstick and choked. They ordered him to get up. Only intervention by neighbors to help him to the cruiser convinced the officers that his leg was broken. In a judgment awarding damages to plaintiff for his injuries, the court stated that the arrest in the middle of the night was imprudent. Plaintiff's identity was known, the crime was trivial and he could have been dealt with the following day. The violence of defendants was unjustified and excessive (68).

Defendants, deputy sheriffs in Wisconsin, went to plaintiff's farm to arrest him for attacking a man with a board. At 1:00 a.m. they arrived and were let into the house. Plaintiff was asleep. They finally aroused him by pinching his nostrils. He responded to their questions with obscenities. They informed plaintiff that he was under arrest for disorderly conduct. Defendants testified that when plaintiff started swinging at them, they struck him in self-defense. Plaintiff's father stated that defendants slapped plaintiff after he was handcuffed, pounded him on the head and face with a flashlight as he lay on the bed, knocked him to the floor, kicked him and dragged him to the cruiser. Plaintiff claimed that he had been awakened by defendants' kicks and blows. Photographs showed a large amount of blood on the bed and floor; medical evidence established that plaintiff had a broken nose. Although the arrest was legal, civil damages were sought for excessive force. The jury rendered a verdict for plaintiff (69).

Denver, Colorado policemen were dispatched to plaintiff's property to settle a disturbance between him and a tenant. He objected, and the officers arrested him for disturbing the peace. A crowd of neighbors gathered. The patrolmen hit plaintiff with their nightsticks to dislodge him and took him to jail. Plaintiff sued them for deprivation of his right to due process of law. An unlawful beating constitutes such denial. The jury decided that the force was unreasonable (70).

FORCE AFTER ARREST

Once an arrestee has been subdued the only force which an

---

68. *Hood v. Brinson,* 30 Ill. App. 2d 498, 175 N.E. 2d 300 (1961).
69. *McCluskey v. Steinhorst,* 45 Wisc. 2d 350, 173 N.W. 2d 148 (1970).
70. *Morgan v. Labiak,* 368 F. 2d 338 (10th Cir. 1966).

officer is privileged to employ is that which is necessary to detain the individual. When additional blows are struck beyond those required to maintain custody, excessive force clearly has been used.

Two officers of Baton Rouge, Louisiana were patroling when a speeding vehicle passed two other cars at an intersection. The police pursued. After several unsuccessful evasive maneuvers, the automobile stopped. Defendant officer went to the operator's door, and his partner approached from the passenger's side. Defendant ordered plaintiff driver to get out. As he slowly complied, he was struck by defendant's nightstick. Plaintiff slumped to his knees and was kicked and hit twice more by defendant. Several occupants of the automobile corroborated plaintiff's testimony. The court did not believe the officer's defense that plaintiff resisted arrest and was the aggressor. This was a traffic arrest; the attack amounted to a deliberate assault upon a person who offered no physical resistance. Defendant was liable. His employer was also responsible, because defendant was acting within the scope and during the course of the employer's business. The employer's knowledge of the employee's intent to commit a wrongful act is not necessary for liability to exist (71).

In the middle of the night plaintiff, while under the influence of alcohol, was speeding in Chicago, Illinois. Two officers arrested him and took him to the station where he was ordered to exhale into a drunkometer to measure his inebriation. When plaintiff refused, they called him a wise guy, battered him with their fists and kicked him. Plaintiff claimed that these blows were intended to punish him for refusal to take the test and sued under the civil rights act. Defendants' motion to dismiss was denied. After this preliminary ruling, the city of Chicago settled by paying damages to plaintiff (72).

UNPROVOKED ATTACK

It is a widespread practice to arrest anyone against whom police exert force, whether or not an offense has been committed. Also,

71. *Taylor v. City of Baton Rouge*, 233 So. 2d 325 (La. App. 1970).
72. *Hardwick v. Hurley*, 289 F. 2d 529 (7th Cir. 1961).

if an arrestee is injured, officers generally file for resisting arrest. These procedures backfire when the arrestee proves that the criminal complaints are a smoke screen for unnecessary violence.

A juvenile alleged that five Cleveland, Ohio officers physically abused him and thereafter filed false charges against him to cover up the assault and battery. Defendant policemen moved to dismiss on the basis that no proper claim under the civil rights statute was made. The court denied the motion (73).

In South Carolina, plaintiff was driving a pickup when defendant constable stopped him. Without provocation, defendant struck plaintiff on the head with a blackjack and then arrested him for three unfounded charges. No defense was presented by defendant. The court awarded both compensatory and punitive damages to plaintiff (74).

Early one night plaintiff, a young man of 23, was having a soft drink with a friend in a Texas tavern. Two officers in civilian clothes entered. One of them approached plaintiff and said, "What is your god damn name?" When he asked who the questioner was, neither policeman identified himself. The other officer retorted, "I don't have to show you a god damn thing." Then he banged plaintiff on the head with either a blackjack or a pistol. Plaintiff fought back, and one policeman grabbed plaintiff's arms while the other pounded his head with a pistol. The young man fell to the ground while the officers kicked him in the throat and face. They took him outside, knocked him down and stomped him in the stomach and shoulder. He was loaded into their vehicle and taken to the hospital. Afterwards he was jailed for drunkenness in a public place. Prosecution was dismissed, and plaintiff sued the policemen for assault. The officers testified that plaintiff incited a barroom brawl, and they exerted only necessary force to arrest him. The evidence supported plaintiff's complaint that the attack was unprovoked and brutal (75).

FORCE BEFORE ARREST OR WITHOUT ARREST

Although officers are privileged to use reasonable force to

73. *Bargainer v. Michal,* 233 F. Supp. 270 (N.D. Ohio 1964).
74. *Brooks v. Moss,* 242 F. Supp. 531 (W.D. S.C. 1965).
75. *Jackson v. Duke,* 259 F. 2d 3 (5 th Cir. 1958).

complete an arrest, they have no right to employ force before an apprehension. When there is no arrest, of course, there will be no exoneration from the consequences of violence.

California policemen pursued two speeding automobiles. The rear speeder collided with the other. Both vehicles and the cruiser stopped. The three occupants of the cars alighted, and the two officers approached them. One patrolman and the driver of the second automobile wrestled. When the operator of the first vehicle attempted to intervene, the other policeman grabbed his arm and held it in an arm lock. His feet were knocked out from under him; he was stomped by both officers and repeatedly hit with a fist. No arrest had been made before the driver was abused. Although he was booked at the station, he was never charged or prosecuted. He suffered severe and permanent injuries from the policeman's blows. In an assault and battery suit against the officer and the city, judgment was awarded to plaintiff driver (76).

One morning while plaintiff was working in her garden in Anchorage, Alaska, two policemen entered her yard. They explained that they had come to talk with her about her son. She answered a few questions and then tired of their inquiries. After she was asked if she had been having trouble with her son lately, she ordered them off the property. They replied that she could not demand that they leave. Plaintiff started screaming; they insisted that she stop or she would be arrested for breach of the peace. One officer grabbed her wrist and twisted her arm. She kicked, scratched and tore his wristwatch off. They knocked her down and pinned her with a knee in her back. She was handcuffed and dragged to the unit. Plaintiff sued the officers for false arrest, false imprisonment, assault and battery. She won compensatory and punitive damages (77).

At about 2:00 a.m. plaintiff went to an apartment house in Dallas, Texas, to visit a friend. Not locating the friend, plaintiff started to go to his car in the parking lot. Defendant, an employee of Great Southwest Patrol, stopped plaintiff and demanded identification. He displayed a driver's license and other cards. The security guard informed plaintiff that he was going to be taken to

76. *Scruggs v. Haynes,* 60 Cal. Rptr. 355 (1967).
77. *Hash v. Hogan,* 453 P.2d 468 (Alaska 1969).

an apartment for a woman to look at him. He was frisked and handcuffed. The apartment dweller denied that he was the man being sought. Defendant called the police inquiring whether plaintiff was wanted for anything, then drew his pistol and ordered plaintiff to a car where he was shoved inside. The guard pointed a shotgun at him and locked the doors. For some 20 minutes defendant stood guard until the city police arrived. They unhandcuffed plaintiff, took him to the station and told him of the suspected charges – peeping tom, burglar and thief. No complaint was filed, and he was released. In a suit against defendant and his employer, plaintiff won on counts of false imprisonment, assault and battery (78).

A New York state trooper investigated a complaint of threatened use of a gun by plaintiff. The incident had occurred in a grill some distance from plaintiff's home. The officer went to the residence and questioned plaintiff outside. When he started into the house, the policeman began to follow. Plaintiff objected to his entering the home without a search warrant; however, the trooper continued behind him. Plaintiff's wife attempted to telephone their attorney, but the officer pushed her against a wall. When plaintiff dialed the lawyer, the trooper grabbed the phone. They scuffled and plaintiff was knocked to the floor and handcuffed. He sued the officer for assault. The court stressed that defendant had no lawful right to enter the home over objection and without a warrant. When defendant struck plaintiff and his wife and interfered with their talking to an attorney, defendant committed an assault (79).

Members of the city council in Reedsburg, Wisconsin considered the zoning of some residential lots at an open meeting. Several citizens, including plaintiff, opposed the measure. Witnesses differed as to whether plaintiff disturbed the session, but the mayor directed defendant policeman to remove plaintiff from the hall. The 278 pound officer picked up the 74 year old plaintiff with one arm behind his neck and carried him to the door. Plaintiff stated that defendant threw him to the sidewalk where he landed face down. Others testified that, as plaintiff and defendant

---

78. *Levine v. Enlow*, 462 S.W. 2d 50 (Tex. 1970).
79. *Frady v. State*, 19 A.D. 2d 783, 242 N.Y.S. 2d 95 (1963).

struggled, plaintiff missed the step outside the door and fell onto the sidewalk. In a suit against defendant and the mayor, the jury found that the latter was not responsible for plaintiff's injuries. Although the mayor's order to remove him was reasonable, the policeman was at fault in using excessive force (80).

ILLEGAL ARREST

An illegal arrest may be resisted with reasonable force. No force is permitted in making an unlawful apprehension; the officer is wrong from the outset. The legality of an arrest is determined at the moment it takes place. If the arrest is legal, it is immaterial for purposes of use of force that a subsequent prosecution fails. If the arrest is unlawful, it is also immaterial if the arrestee is subsequentlv found guilty.

Late one night defendant, a Rhode Island policeman, was walking his beat when his attention was attracted by plaintiff making faces and sticking out his tongue at defendant. Plaintiff was inside a poolroom. Defendant spoke to plaintiff and then resumed his patrol. After a distance of twenty to thirty yards separated them, plaintiff shouted at defendant. The language used was not profane or obscene. Defendant returned and arrested plaintiff. There was some resistance to the apprehension. No evidence was presented as to the charges filed or the outcome of the prosecution. Plaintiff sued for false arrest, assault and battery. Because there was no justification for the arrest, plaintiff won on both counts (81).

Two Louisiana officers overheard a police radio transmission about a fight at a bar between plaintiff and the younger brother of defendant policeman. They finished their tour of duty, returned their cruiser and left the station in defendant's personal car. They were still in uniform and wearing sidearms. Enroute home they stopped at the bar. When asked about the fight, the brother said that it was over and that he and plaintiff were friends. As defendant turned to leave, plaintiff made a remark which defendant interpreted as insulting. Defendant informed plaintiff

80. *Schulze v. Kleeber,* 10 Wisc. 2d 540, 103 N.W. 2d 560 (1960).
81. *Tessier v. La Nois,* 198 A. 2d 142 (R.I. 1964).

that he was under arrest. Plaintiff went peacefully to defendant's car. After they had driven about five blocks, defendant stopped and ordered plaintiff outside. They started fighting. Plaintiff was seriously injured even though the fracas lasted only thirty seconds. Immediately afterwards, plaintiff was ordered into the automobile and driven home. He was not taken to jail; no charges were preferred against him.

Plaintiff sued both policemen and the city's liability insurer. The partner officer was exonerated because he did not participate in the arrest or fighting. Defendant was liable. Responsibility of the insurer was based on the fact that defendant was acting within the scope of his employment when he hurt plaintiff. Although defendant had finished his shift, he was empowered to perform police activities at all times. Plaintiff was told that he was under arrest and was in custody when the assault and battery took place (82).

Sears Roebuck and Company contracted with a private detective agency for guard service at its store in Detroit, Michigan. One of the guards responded to a call from the lingerie department where he was told that a customer had stuffed some merchandise into a shopping bag and departed without paying. The saleslady accompanied him to the door and pointed out plaintiff on the sidewalk. Plaintiff had loose articles in her arms. When he demanded to see receipts, she produced only one. He tried to take her back to the store. She refused, hit him with an umbrella and started off. He shoved her to the pavement, straddled her and pinned her arms down. A crowd gathered, and the police arrived. They discovered that the shoplifting charge was baseless. She sued the guard, the agency and Sears for false arrest, assault and battery. All were liable (83).

A motorist reported to the New York state police that an object had been hurled at his windshield while he was traveling on the thruway. No other vehicle was close to the motorist when the damage occurred, and no persons were observed near the highway. Defendant trooper was taken to the site of the incident, not far from plaintiff's home. The officer climbed an incline and went

82. *Bourque v. Lohr,* 248 So. 2d 901 (La. App. 1971).
83. *Nash v. Sears Roebuck & Co.,* 12 Mich. App. 553, 163 N.W. 2d 471 (1969).

over a fence where he saw some trodden snow and footprints leading to a residence. He knocked on the door. Plaintiff husband appeared at a side entrance. Defendant went inside past him into the living room where plaintiff wife, eight months pregnant, was undergoing a heat lamp treatment. She was only partially clad. After interrogating both plaintiffs, the officer inspected their car and demanded that the husband leave with him. At no time did defendant explain why he was there or what he was investigating. The husband resisted, and a fight broke out between the officer and plaintiffs. The trooper told the husband that he was under arrest but did not explain the charges. Plaintiff called the police, and three other officers arrived. Defendant filed charges on both plaintiffs. When the grand jury heard the evidence, no true bill was issued. Plaintiffs sued defendant for assault and battery, false arrest, false imprisonment and malicious prosecution. Defendant had no grounds for arresting plaintiffs. They resisted an unlawful arrest with reasonable force. The court ruled for plaintiffs (84).

CONCLUSION

Police brutality claims usually take the form of assault and battery. Courts scrutinize such complaints in the light of the presumption that the officer acted properly and exerted only the force necessary under the circumstances. In aggravated cases plaintiffs will recover. However, judges and juries are loathe to second guess a law enforcer who demonstrates that he behaved reasonably in a trying situation.

84. *Powell v. State,* 191 N.Y.S. 2d 846 (1959).

CHAPTER EIGHT

TEAR GAS

TO satisfy a need for effective nonlethal weapons, law enforcement has rushed into equipping members with tear gas. Anxiety over civil disturbances and demands for intermediate tools between a nightstick and a revolver have led to uncritical adoption of these devices. However, the F.B.I. and numerous agencies reevaluated the hazard and no longer issue tear gas dispensers. The fact that some departments have determined that these instrumentalities are excessively dangerous gives litigants an argument that other organizations should act accordingly.

Warnings that accompany tear gas containers often do not filter down to the man in the field. If he is not notified, or if the instructions are not explained and stressed, he may not employ the weapon correctly. When arrested victims of tear gas are denied prompt aid to alleviate pain and mitigate permanent injuries, the aggravation of their misery may result in liability.

Many doctors have vigorously protested the widespread utilization of tear gas. They emphasize the harm to eyes which, in addition to pain and tearing, may include scarring, corneal opacity and loss of vision. Also, injury to other parts of the body is frequent. If the gas is discharged directly on the skin, severe burns may occur. Firing into a small enclosed room causes the victim to breathe the substance. Serious deterioration of the respiratory system or death may follow. Many dispensers such as tear gas pens and gas billies, spew fragments of solid chemical, metal and wadding as well as the irritating gas. At close range these objects may cause extreme damage.

Sellers have soft-pedaled the hazards and exaggerated the safety. Some devices are dangerous even when used according to directions. Other types cause permanent damage only when improperly fired. Manufacturers have been successfully sued for defective and inherently dangerous products. Generally, if the container is properly labeled and appropriate instructions for use are included, the seller will have a valid defense; the burden of litigation will fall upon supervisors and officers.

Tear gas devices must be regarded as an extreme amount of force. At times, they have a place in the police arsenal. In situations in which ultimate force is necessary, tear gas is a suitable alternative. If treated as a dangerous instrument just short of a firearm, this weapon will be used more wisely than it has been in the past.

MISCELLANEOUS TEAR GAS WEAPONS

Plaintiff sued both an Iowa town and a marshal for injuries sustained when he was shot with a tear gas gun while being arrested. He contended that tear gas was not needed. Fault of the town was based upon its equipping the officer with this weapon. But the town was dismissed as a defendant because it was not irresponsible in furnishing the officer with this tool. The liability of the marshal will be ascertained upon a hearing of the facts (85).

While plaintiff was in an Arizona bar, defendant deputy sheriff arrested him for disturbing the peace. Defendant fired a tear gas gun, from a distance of approximately three feet, into plaintiff's face. He became helpless. Defendant pulled him out of the hall and jailed him without rendering first aid. No one assisted plaintiff in caring for his eyes until he was taken to the hospital the next morning. Plaintiff sued the deputy, the sheriff and his surety and recovered from all three. The sheriff had issued the weapon to defendant; instructions as to its use had been received under the sheriff's supervision. The dispersal of the tear gas was excessive force and constituted a wanton and reckless assault upon plaintiff (86).

The New York state police received a complaint from a contractor concerning broken windshields on some cars belonging to his employees. A trooper went to the only house remaining in the immediate area to question the occupants. The other buildings

85. *Hagedorn v. Schrum*, 226 Iowa 128 (1939).
86. *Chaudoin v. Fuller*, 76 Ariz. 144, 192 P. 2d 243 (1948).

had been demolished in preparation for highway construction. A mother and son in the house were interviewed. They denied any knowledge of the broken windshields, but the boy said that his 29 year old brother may have been involved. The latter refused to talk with the officer or to leave the bedroom. The mother and brother explained that the son had been upset over pending destruction of their home and loss of a newspaper route that he had maintained for years. He had finished grade school and one month of high school and was unemployed except for the delivery service. Recently he had become a virtual recluse, locking himself in his room and refusing to shave or have a haircut.

The trooper suggested getting the town health officer to examine the son for possible commitment. The trooper left to find the doctor, an ambulance and other policemen. Upon returning he and a fellow policeman unsuccessfully tried to coax the son from his room. They broke the lock and forced the door, only to have it slammed shut. When it was reopened, a bumper jack, hammer and chair were thrown at them, and the entrance was barricaded. Six officers had arrived. The next tactic to rout the son was tear gas. A grenade was fired into the room. Because of the barricaded door and the absence of gas masks, the troopers were unable to enter the room for several minutes. Finally the limp body of the son was reached. He was moaning and frothing at the mouth. The ambulance rushed him to the hospital where he died some fourteen hours later.

His mother sued the state, which employed the troopers, and won. The bedroom into which the grenade had been fired was 9 feet by 9 feet and 8 feet 6 inches high. Experts testified that a deadly concentration of gas was formed within five minutes. The type of canister used was designed for the control of outside crowds and not for indoors. The police contended that decedent had assaulted them by throwing objects at them. However, the court pointed out that this was legal resistance to attempted illegal entry into the room. It was not proper for the police to remove decedent from his room to decide if he were mentally competent. The state was at fault in not instructing the officers that tear gas could be lethal. They were negligent in failing to bring gas masks (87).

87. *Titcomb v. State,* 30 Misc. 2d 902, 222 N.Y.S. 2d 596 (1961).

TEAR GAS PEN

Defendant, a village sergeant in West Virginia, arrested plaintiff for drunkenness and disorderly conduct. Although he did not resist arrest, defendant deliberately fired a small tear gas gun near plaintiff's face causing him to lose the sight of his left eye. The weapon, appearing to be an ordinary fountain pen, was discharged by pressing a button on the side. The usual range of this device is from 15 to 20 feet. The jury found that firing at such close range was excessive force and held both the sergeant and his surety liable for plaintiff's injury. Upon appeal, the court reversed because the jury instructions had not clearly spelled out that reasonable force must be determined in the light of the attending circumstances and that an officer is presumed to act in good faith as to the force employed (88).

Late one night defendant, a North Dakota officer, was patroling when he observed a Volkswagen parked near an abandoned house. Upon investigating the vehicle, he found plaintiff asleep or unconscious in the back seat. The motor was running, and plaintiff was grasping an open can of beer in his hand. Defendant removed the can, roused plaintiff and told him that he could not sleep there. When plaintiff refused to budge, they scuffled. Plaintiff had decided to spend the night in his car; he was parked on his mother's property. Defendant did not know who plaintiff was or why he was there. The area was dark, and plaintiff did not realize that defendant was a policeman. Plaintiff, who had been knocked down, got up and ran into the house. While chasing plaintiff, defendant removed a tear gas pen from his uniform and took it off the safety position. He carried a flashlight in his other hand. Plaintiff went to the far end of the house; defendant grabbed him by the arm. As they fought, the tear gas gun discharged near plaintiff's eyes and blinded him.

Defendant contended that he had arrested plaintiff for vagrancy; plaintiff resisted and attempted to escape. In the struggle to take plaintiff into custody, the projectile accidentally fired. Plaintiff showed that defendant had a history of mental problems and treatment in several mental hospitals. He had been

---

88. *Village of Barboursville ex rel. Bates v. Taylor,* 115 W. Va. 4, 174 S.E. 485, 92 A.L.R. 1093 (1934).

discharged from military service for mental instability and was on a pension from another police department because of mental and physical disabilities. The jury rendered a verdict for plaintiff, which was reversed and a new trial granted because of errors in instructions. It was erroneous for the court to instruct the jury that the tear gas fountain pen was a firearm. Although it may be regarded as a dangerous weapon if discharged within three feet of a person and aimed at his eyes, it is not perilous when used properly. Also, instructions were incorrect that the officer has the burden of proving that he did not use unnecessary force; plaintiff must establish that the force was unreasonable (89).

TEAR GAS BILLIES

Suits against manufacturers of tear gas billies have been successful. Whether or not the maker warns law enforcers of the hazards of the product, probably future verdicts will be won against the police for use of this device. They will be assumed to know that gas billies are dangerous instrumentalities.

Plaintiff, a 24 year old incorrigible prisoner in maximum detention at the South Carolina State Prison, was fighting with a guard and creating a disturbance. The guard had refused to let plaintiff spend his alloted time in the prison yard. Plaintiff was severely beating up the guard when the warden intervened with a gas billy in hand. He held it near the inmate's waist. Plaintiff jolted the weapon toward his face as he swung at the guard. At that moment the warden discharged the billy. Plaintiff was totally and permanently blinded. In a suit against the manufacturer, experts testified that the blast expulsion method of disseminating the gas from the billy was intolerably perilous for its expected use. The weapon expelled solid particles of gas, inert carrier metal, gunpowder, wadding and a metal primer cap at a speed of several hundred miles per hour. Blindness could result from its being fired at almost any recommended distance. Also, flaming gases could inflict severe burns at close range. The manufacturer advertised that the weapon was suitable for nearby targets without disclosing

89. *Wall v. Zeeb,* 153 N.W. 2d 779 (N.D. 1967).

any of the hazards (90).

A Pennsylvania borough cruiser was delivered to a radio repairman for service. The officer to whom the unit was assigned left his issued gas billy, loaded and cocked, hanging from the cigarette lighter. The vehicle was taken to the repairman's home for the radio work. While it was there, the repairman's thirteen year old son explored the interior. He saw the gas billy and, assuming that it was a flashlight, attempted to shine it on the equipment underneath the dashboard. When the billy would not light, he turned it toward his face. It exploded causing permanent impairment of his vision. Neither the boy nor his father had been cautioned by the policeman that the billy was in the unit or that it was a dangerous instrument. A suit against the officer, his department and the manufacturer of the gas billy was settled for a substantial sum (91).

CONCLUSION

Although tear gas is not a new weapon to law enforcers, its use has expanded in the past several years. Few lawsuits have been filed by gas victims because most of them are only temporarily harmed. However, when damages are serious and permanent, victims sue. If tear gas has been improperly used or the victim's injuries have been aggravated by failure to render first aid, plaintiffs generally win.

90. *Ussery v. Fed. Lab., Inc.,* F. Supp. (D.S.C. 1972).
91. *Landfried v. Fed. Lab., Inc.,* (Ct. Comm. Pls., Allegheny Co. Pa. 1969).

CHAPTER NINE

FALSE ARREST, FALSE IMPRISONMENT AND MALICIOUS PROSECUTION

THE torts of false arrest, false imprisonment and malicious prosecution will be discussed together because often all three are filed as separate counts arising from an incident. However, they are separate torts and have distinct elements. If there is an illegal arrest, false imprisonment results from the unlawful custody. But false imprisonment may follow a legal arrest when the justification for detention is no longer present. Malicious prosecution need not exist in any of these situations.

Illegal arrests may be made with or without a warrant. Ordinarily, when an officer makes an illegal arrest pursuant to a warrant that is valid on its face, he is immune from personal liability. He is regarded as an arm of the court performing orders. However, if the warrant is patently defective or the policeman does not exercise reasonable care to arrest the proper person, there may be liability.

In a suit for false arrest based upon an apprehension without a warrant, no such immunity protects the law enforcer. Also, he has the burden of proving justification for his act. He must establish probable cause for the arrest. If the case involves a misdemeanor, usually it must have been committed in his presence to authorize him to arrest without a warrant. For a felony, the officer must have probable cause to believe that the crime was committed by the arrestee. These are the general rules. Some states have modified them by specific statutes relating to particular offenses. The test in determining if an arrest is legal is the existence of probable cause at the moment of the arrest. Whether the person is or is not convicted is irrelevant. Obviously, many legal apprehensions result in dismissals or not guilty verdicts for reasons which have nothing to do with the officer's work at the inception of the case.

False imprisonment means unauthorized restraint, whether the individual is kept in an open street, a moving vehicle or a police station. Restraint may be imposed by physical barriers, threats or the assertion of legal authority. However, one is not falsely imprisoned if he voluntarily agrees to confinement, such as by freely accompanying an officer for questioning. Consent is an affirmative defense which the officer must prove. Persons do not always know that they can refuse detention. Awareness of the right not to comply is a significant element of consent.

False imprisonment may arise from failure to release an inmate from custody at the end of his sentence or when the reason for confinement no longer exists. Detention following an illegal arrest is always contrary to law. Thus, whenever there is false arrest, there is also false imprisonment. But false imprisonment may follow a valid apprehension.

The elements of malicious prosecution are as follows: 1) criminal charges filed or continued by defendant against plaintiff, 2) termination of the proceedings in favor of plaintiff, 3) lack of probable cause for the charges and 4) malice. All of these must be proven by petitioner. Defendant may defeat element [2] by showing that plaintiff is guilty of the crime, even though he was acquitted or the case was not prosecuted. Merely demonstrating that defendant had ill will or hatred toward plaintiff is not sufficient to establish malice.

Both false arrest and malicious prosecution take into account the motives of the defendant. In the former the stress and urgency of the encounter are considered to mitigate the fault while in the latter the deliberateness of the actions are an element of plaintiff's case. Motives are not material in false imprisonment. If the facts constitute illegal detention, the tort is complete. Malicious prosecution arises only when defendant had proceeded under proper legal formalities; false arrest and false imprisonment are based upon a departure from due process of law.

PROBABLE CAUSE FOR ARREST

The legality of an arrest without a warrant depends upon whether the officer had probable cause to believe that the person committed the offense for which he is arrested. It is not sufficient for the policeman to be suspicious of an individual. Holding one for investigation or on open charges is illegal. Probable cause has been defined by the United States Supreme Court to be a reasonable belief that the arrestee is the violator. The only way to understand this circuitous definition is by examining how it works in actual situations. A couple of fundamentals to probable cause are: 1) the facts are evaluated at the moment of arrest; later acquired information is not pertinent and 2) hearsay data is allowed to the extent that it is reliable.

Shortly before 3:00 p.m., a bank was robbed at gunpoint in Elm Creek, Nebraska. A bank employee described the robber as Larry Wilson, 25 years old, 5 feet 10 inches, 165 pounds, dark complexion, dark eyes, black hair and believed to be living in Lexington or Cozad. The information was broadcast to all officers. A vehicle registration check showed a Larry Wilson residing in Lexington. A state trooper was told that Larry Wilson in Lexington was the wanted subject. Another officer joined the trooper at Wilson's residence. They saw him inside and entered the house. When they asked where he had been for the last hour, he replied that he had just returned from Elm Creek. Larry explained that he had been to Elm Creek to collect a bill for his father. They handcuffed him and led him to the cruiser. Larry and his mother testified that the officers entered without invitation, pointed guns at him and dragged him to the patrol car. The trooper stated that he removed his revolver from the holster. The other policeman said that he did not draw a weapon. Larry walked between the officers to the vehicle. They helped him across the yard because he was in his stocking feet and stepped on sandburrs. The trooper radioed his supervisor who told him to remain at the Wilson residence. Within a few minutes the sergeant arrived. He informed them that they had the wrong man, unfastened the handcuffs and released Larry. The description of the robber fit Larry closely except for a difference of five years in age.

Larry sued for false arrest, false imprisonment and assault and battery. The court determined that the officers had probable cause for the arrest. The detention of about 15 minutes was reasonable after the lawful arrest. Although one of the officers pointed a gun at Larry, this was not improper in apprehending a suspected armed robber. Handcuffing to protect the policemen and prevent escape was a recognized procedure. Evidence of undue force in dragging Larry to the car was flimsy in view of Larry's admission that he was not abused. Judgment was for defendants (92).

Plaintiff sued six Wisconsin policemen for deprivation of constitutional rights in a homicide investigation arising from death of a fellow employee during a robbery of a gas station. Three days after the crime, city detectives asked plaintiff if he would accompany them to headquarters and answer some questions. He agreed. About two hours later, when he thought that the interview had ended, he got up to leave. He was told to remain. Some hours later, having taken two lie detector tests, he was informed that he was under arrest. The next day he was taken to Madison to the crime lab and given another polygraph examination. He went voluntarily in the hope that the test would clear him. Afterwards he was returned and released. There was no prosecution.

Plaintiff grounded his civil claim upon being arrested without a warrant, detained for 18 or 19 hours after formal arrest, not taken promptly to a magistrate and then freed without prosecution. Plaintiff's recovery depended upon whether defendants had probable cause for the arrest and whether the length of detention was reasonable. The court ruled that probable cause existed, and the detention was acceptable in view of the circumstances, including plaintiff's admitted willingness to journey to Madison. A verdict was directed for defendants. The officers had probable cause for the arrest on the basis of the following facts. Plaintiff was a fellow employee of decedent; two men thought they saw him at the gas station sometime close to the time of the crime; an old model Plymouth such as one driven by plaintiff was observed leaving the area by the policeman who investigated the robbery; plaintiff mentioned that he heard of the incident and the name of the decedent on the radio the morning after the shooting, but the announcer did not broadcast the name of decedent or place of death; plaintiff had told his employer a week before the crime that he carried a .22 caliber revolver in his car, and this type of weapon

92. *Wilson v. Gutschenritter,* 185 Neb. 311, 175 N.W. 2d 282 (1970).

was used in the murder (93).

Policemen were summoned to a bar in Santa Monica, California to investigate an incident. Decedent, after having been struck twice in the face by plaintiff, landed on the floor with a thud and lay there in a semiconscious condition. Plaintiff said that he acted in self-defense after the fellow pulled a pen knife. Only decedent was taken to the station. While he was standing next to the booking desk, he stiffened with a sudden seizure and fell over backwards. He was rushed in an ambulance to the hospital where he died a few hours later. Doctors concluded that death resulted from the blows and fall at the bar. The officer talked with an eyewitness, who stated that plaintiff had assaulted her and torn some buttons on her blouse; then, without any provocation, he had knocked decedent down. A few hours later one of the policemen met plaintiff and asked him to come to headquarters for questioning. He volunteered to accompany the officer. During the interview, plaintiff changed his story. He now denied that deceased had pulled a knife on him and admitted hitting deceased with his fists. After about one-half hour of interrogation, plaintiff was arrested for murder. He was convicted of involuntary manslaughter, but the verdict was reversed upon appeal because of erroneous jury instructions. Prosecution was dismissed.

Plaintiff sued the officers for deprivation of due process. In ruling for defendants the court stated that the arrest was based upon probable cause and did not violate plaintiff's rights. No arrest occurred until defendants had talked with an eyewitness, had received medical opinion that death was caused by the blows and fall at the bar, and had heard plaintiff make statements inconsistent with prior answers (94).

A black female selected some groceries at a supermarket in Phoenix, Arizona. She presented a check for $113.47. After a telephone inquiry about the validity of the check, the store refused it. By the time it was sent back to the customer, she had fled. A stock boy had followed her and recorded the make, model and license number of her car. The registered owner was a woman with a local address. Similar forged checks were being passed by a

93. *Thornton v. Buchmann,* 392 F. 2d 870 (7th Cir. 1968).
94. *Hebert v. Morley,* 273 F. Supp. 800 (C.D. Cal. 1967).

group of Negroes. Drivers license photographs of acquaintances of the ringleader were given to the investigating officer. He selected four of five pictures of Negro women from the stack; however, no photograph of the woman who owned the escape vehicle was included in those displayed. Some three weeks after the incident, the policeman exhibited these photographs to various store personnel. The manager identified plaintiff. Almost a month later the officer swore out a warrant for plaintiff's arrest on the basis of the manager's identification. There were no other grounds to connect plaintiff with the case. At the preliminary hearing the complaint was dismissed because a key witness failed to appear. Nearly three months later, again founded only on the manager's statement, the policeman filed another complaint. Plaintiff was apprehended. Preliminary hearing, more than nine months later, led to dismissal.

Plaintiff sued for malicious prosecution and won against the officer and the city. Criminal charges had been filed because of one identification; others to whom the licenses were shown did not pick out plaintiff. No effort was made to include among the photographs an obvious suspect: the owner of the escape vehicle. No investigation was conducted as to plaintiff's whereabouts at the time of the crime. She was not interviewed as to the crime. No lineup was held. The chief of the department, qualified as an expert on police procedure, testified that Caucasians, such as the manager, are not able to identify blacks as accurately as they can identify whites, that recognition in person is more reliable than from photographs, and that the automobile owner was a valid suspect. Plaintiff has been a resident of Arizona for twenty-one years; there was no indication, to justify arresting her, that she planned to flee. The prosecution was initiated without probable cause and with malice (95).

Plaintiffs, members of a group of white and black Episcopal clergymen, were on a tour of the country. During a stop at Jackson, Mississippi, they went to a bus terminal waiting room which was marked "for whites only by order of the police department." They planned to enter a small restaurant, but they

95. *Watzek v. Walker,* 14 Ariz. App. 545, 485 P. 2d 3 (1971).

were told to move on by two officers. When they refused, they were arrested for breach of the peace. All were convicted, but the judgments were reversed on appeal. Plaintiffs sued the policemen under the civil rights act for false arrest. Subsequent to the arrest, the breach of the peace statute was held unconstitutional. The officers defended on the basis that the apprehensions were made in good faith and upon probable cause. The United States Supreme Court ruled that if the policemen could prove these contentions they would have a valid defense (96).

Thirteen plaintiffs sued nineteen defendants in the New Mexico federal court for violation of civil rights. The plaintiffs were members or relatives of affiliates of an organization of Spanish-Americans who sought to recapture lands, take over local government and establish their own system. The defendants were the district attorney, fifteen state policemen and three National Guardsmen. After two mass meetings over a period of about one month, a group assembled at a ranch. From there several car loads of men, women and children armed with guns, dynamite and knives set out for the courthouse. They seized it for approximately two hours. Numerous shots were fired, public officials were wounded and kidnapped before the insurrectionists fled back to the ranch. Many state policemen followed. Upon learning of the raid, the acting governor called out the National Guard. Persons at the ranch were interviewed in small groups. Some of the raiders were arrested; others had disappeared. Nonraiders were permitted to return to their campsites at the ranch. National Guardsmen kept watch for about 24 hours before the campers left. They were not formally arrested or detained. The jury decided against 12 plaintiffs. The winning claim of the thirteenth related to illegal search of his home without a warrant for the ringleader several days after the incident.

The twelve appealed, partly on the basis that the trial judge erroneously instructed the jury that the standards for arrest which apply to National Guardsmen are not the same as those for policemen. Verdict for defendants was affirmed. The governor is the sole determiner of whether the military arm of the state shall

---

96. *Pierson v. Ray,* 386 U.S. 547, 18 L. Ed. 2d 288, 87 S. Ct. 1213 (1967).

be activated. When ordered into service, the National Guard commander may seize persons who stand in the way of restoring peace. Such arrests are not necessarily for punishment, but are a precaution to prevent hostility. If such custody is in good faith and in the honest belief that it was necessary under the circumstances to preserve peace, there is no liability. Any arrests or detention by the state police must be founded upon probable cause. The jury decided for defendant officers under proper instruction regarding probable cause and for defendant National Guardsmen under correct law that probable cause did not apply to them (97).

LEGALITY OF ARREST CANCELED

Sometimes arrests that appear legal at the time lose their validity because of other factors. For example, when an individual is entrapped into committing a crime, his arrest is illegal. The apprehension would be valid except for the improper acts of the entrappers. These acts cancel the legality of the arrest and leave the apprehenders vulnerable to charges of false arrest and imprisonment.

Plaintiff, a merchant in California, was leaving his store to attend the races when a stranger came in to see him. The visitor represented himself to be a friend and employee of a person whom plaintiff knew. After the stranger asked plaintiff if he were going to the track, the visitor asked plaintiff to place a ten dollar bet on a horse in the fifth race. Plaintiff invited the man to join him for the races. When the visitor said that he had to work, plaintiff agreed to make the bet. He walked out the back door and was met by an officer who said that he was under arrest for bookmaking. The stranger was a deputy sheriff. He and the policeman explained that the chief had told them to arrest plaintiff. The officers asserted that the arrest was legal; a felony had been committed and there was probable cause to believe that plaintiff was the felon. At the prosecution he was found not guilty because of entrapment.

---

97. *Valdez v. Black,* 446 F.2d 1071 (10th Cir. 1971).

He sued the chief and the two officers for false arrest and imprisonment in a state court. At a hearing on a motion to dismiss the merchant showed that none of the defendants had any knowledge that he was engaged in bookmaking, or any other criminal activity, before the incident in question. Their only basis for the arrest was the crime which plaintiff had been entrapped into committing. Therefore, the court ruled that the arrest was unlawful as without probable cause and denied the motion (98).

The case was removed from state to federal court for civil trial. The federal court refused to accept plaintiff's version of the facts and relied upon the officers' testimony. Therefore, it upheld the arrest as founded upon probable cause. Even though the chief's acts were motivated by malice and personal bias against plaintiff, the arrest was legal and defendants prevailed (99).

Defendant, deputy sheriff of Los Angeles, California, was assigned to serve warrants sent to him by the main office. He received a stack of about a dozen warrants, one of which was directed against plaintiff, of whom the deputy had never heard. Upon examination, he noted that the warrant was twelve years old and was for the misdemeanor of malicious mischief. Since the warrant had been given to him, he concluded that it was valid and that he was obligated to carry out its command. He went to plaintiff's home and arrested him. Plaintiff was booked and confined two days. When he was brought before a judge, the case was dismissed because it involved a minor offense which occurred more than twelve years earlier. Plaintiff sued the deputy. His defense was that the warrant was regular on its face, and he was immune from civil liability for serving it. The court ruled that the age of the misdemeanor warrant rendered it invalid. There was no justification for serving a warrant bearing a date that had passed so long before because no prosecution could be based upon it. However, the court refused to hold the deputy liable. He acted in good faith reliance upon the validity of the warrant. Whether a warrant that was regular on its face when issued loses its regularity by passage of time was a complex legal question which the deputy

98. *Beauregard v. Wingard,* 237 Cal. App. 2d 760, 47 Cal. Rptr. 279, 15 A.L.R. 3d 955 (1965).
99. *Beauregard v. Wingard,* 362 F. 2d 901 (9th Cir. 1966).

should not have been required to answer at his peril (100).

ARREST OF WRONG PERSON

The Pennsylvania state police asked the Cleveland, Ohio police department to check confidentially if a named and described individual resided at a certain place. Cleveland police investigated and replied that the person was living at the address and described the vehicle that he was said to be operating. The Pennsylvania agency requested that he be picked up on a forgery warrant. Local officers arrested plaintiff, who denied that he was the one wanted. The following morning a fugitive warrant was issued by a Pennsylvania court. Plaintiff was released after posting bond, and the case was continued for ten days to allow the state to bring extradition proceedings. A complete description of plaintiff plus a photograph and fingerprints were forwarded to Pennsylvania authorities. When they determined that he was not the man wanted, the case was dismissed.

Plaintiff sued the local officers for false arrest and false imprisonment. The court held that they acted properly and were not at fault. A sister state identified plaintiff by address and name except for a variance in the middle initial. He had recently come to Ohio from Pennsylvania. Before the apprehension an investigative report was sent to Pennsylvania. That state then requested the arrest upon the basis of a warrant. Plaintiff did not precisely fit the physical description given by Pennsylvania, but the difference was not so great as to make defendants' actions unreasonable (101).

An individual cashed a worthless check at a hotel in Albuquerque, New Mexico. The proprietors complained to defendant, deputy sheriff, who obtained an arrest warrant. This was taken to the district attorney together with a written description of the check passer. A city policeman arrested a person of the same name at his place of business and confined him to jail. The arrestee, plaintiff, was not comparable in size or physical appearance to the man described by the hotel personnel and was not the one who

100. *Quinette v. Garland,* 277 F. Supp. 999 (C. D. Cal. 1967).
101. *Johnson v. Reddy,* 113 Ohio St. 347, 126 N.E. 2d 911 (1955).

issued the checks. After dismissal of the criminal charges, plaintiff sued the city, sheriff, deputy and the original complainants. All of them except the deputy were released as defendants. The successful defense of the city was governmental immunity. The sheriff prevailed upon a legal technicality. The citizens were not at fault because they, in good faith and with probable cause, swore out a criminal complaint identifying the accused by name. They were not responsible for the arrest of a person by that name who was not the culprit. The deputy's liability depends upon whether he exercised reasonable care to arrest the proper person. The fact that plaintiff did not fit the description of the accused individual indicated that the deputy did not do so (102).

A New York state trooper stopped a vehicle which was being operated on the wrong side of the center line. The motorist identified herself by name but said that her driver's license was at home on a nearby Indian reservation. The officer replied that he would follow her home to see her license. The reservation is adjacent to the Canadian border. As she neared the border, she accelerated and crossed. He could not follow. Four days later he filed two complaints against her, for the center line violation and operating without a license. Warrants were issued. A couple of weeks later two other troopers were told to arrest a woman in a bar on the warrants. They had no description of the accused. About twenty-five people were in the lounge when they approached plaintiff and asked if her name were the one listed on the warrants. The name was common in the area. She replied that this was her maiden name; however, she was married and had a different surname. She was apprehended and taken to a justice of the peace some seven or eight miles distance. During the trip she asked about the arrest. At least two or three times she denied that she was the accused. One officer asked for her driver's license. She did not have it with her. At the court she again stated that they had the wrong person. Before she could make bond, she was kept in jail for about two days. During her incarceration she was twice interrogated about other crimes. A hearing was held a week after her release. The trooper who filed the complaint testified that

102. *Barnett v. Cal M, Inc.*, 79 N.M. 533, 445 P.2d 974 (1968).

plaintiff was not the accused, and the charges were dismissed.

She successfully sued the state, as employer of the officers, for false arrest and false imprisonment. An officer must exercise reasonable care to satisfy himself that he has seized the proper person. The troopers were first told that plaintiff used a different surname although her maiden name was the one inquired about; then she repeatedly denied being the accused. They had no description of the suspect. The only effort to establish the validity of the arrest was to ask for a driver's license, and she had none with her. They did not use due diligence to find out if they were arresting the correct person (103).

BAD FAITH SHOWN BY OFFICER'S PRIOR DEALINGS

Good faith and probable cause to believe that the proper party is being arrested amount to a valid defense to claims of false arrest. Bad faith can be demonstrated by the officer's prior dealings with the arrestee or his awareness that the statute upon which the apprehension is based is inapplicable.

Plaintiff was in itinerant vendor who took orders for tailored clothing which after manufacture was shipped directly to the customer. On two previous occasions plaintiff had been arrested in a small New Mexico town for violation of a city ordinance imposing an occupational tax. He had been fined both times and had won appeals of the convictions. He claimed immunity from the ordinance on the basis that he was engaged in interstate commerce. Defendant, a local policeman, was notified that plaintiff was breaking the ordinance. Defendant witnessed plaintiff measure a prospective customer and, without a warrant, arrested plaintiff. He sued for wrongful arrest and imprisonment. The policeman could not rely in good faith on the applicability of the ordinance on this third arrest, because twice before plaintiff had had his convictions under the ordinance reversed. The court refused defendant's argument that he acted under a privilege of enforcing an ordinance that was valid on its face (104).

---

103. *Maracle v. State,* 50 Misc. 2d 348, 270 N.Y.S. 2d 439 (1966).

104. *Miller v. Stinnett,* 257 F. 2d 910 (10th Cir. 1958).

Plaintiff was the dean of men and a sociologist at a midwestern college. As part of the scholastic program, he often took pupils on field trips. In the spring semester, he traveled with ten students to Alabama to study nonviolent techniques. The day after arrival, they interviewed members of a black organization. At lunchtime the entire assemblage adjourned to a cafe in a black neighborhood. They went into a private dining room from which they could neither see out nor could those on the outside see in. When they entered, activity was minimal on the street in front of the restaurant.

Shortly before noon an anonymous person reported to the police that young white girls were going into the cafe with blacks. An officer, dispatched to the scene, observed an orderly group having lunch. The policeman notified his superiors. A crowd was forming in the street. The peaceful gathering inside the dining room was not told that they had to leave or that they were violating the law before the chief arrested and jailed them. At the time of the arrests, crowds of 50 to 150 blacks were in the streets and cars filled with whites congested the area. Plaintiff and his wife were released on bail late in the afternoon. The next morning warrants were issued for plaintiff and his companions for disorderly conduct in violation of a city ordinance. At trial everyone was convicted. Upon appeal, the judgments were reversed.

Plaintiff sued for false imprisonment and malicious prosecution. The court held that the arrest and imprisonment were unlawful. The policemen knew of the repeal of ordinances enforcing segregation in public places, including cafes. The present ordinance on disorderly conduct did not pertain to segregation; it referred to disturbing the peace. Plaintiff and his associates were merely eating lunch with blacks. This was not a breach of the peace. The only threat of disorder was outside the restaurant where crowds were assembled. Three of the necessary four elements of malicious prosecution unquestionably existed: 1) a criminal proceeding instituted by defendants, 2) termination of the prosecution in favor of the accused and 3) absence of probable cause for the arrest. The fourth element, malice, may be inferred from lack of probable cause, but this is a jury question and cannot be decided as a matter of law by a court. The trial judge erroneously refused to submit this matter to the jury. On appeal the verdict was reversed and the case remanded for retrial on the issues of malice and damages, actual and punitive. The claim for false imprisonment and the first three elements of malicious prosecution were decided as matters of law for plaintiff by the appellate judge (105).

Plaintiff claimed that on three occasions over a two year period he was arrested and imprisoned in deprivation of his constitutional rights by members of a Colorado police department. The first time related to a complaint that he had short-changed some children who purchased ice cream from him. He was taken into custody and locked in a cell for five hours with several other prisoners before being released without prosecution. A few weeks later two policemen came to his home and asked him to accompany them to headquarters. Upon inquiry they replied that they did not know why he was wanted. At the station he was questioned for two hours about molesting a ten year old girl. He was freed without being charged. Other testimony established that the offense never occurred. The third occasion was an arrest to interrogate plaintiff about a burglary. He was jailed overnight and then dismissed without charges. No warrants against plaintiff were issued in any of the incidents. He asserted that each time he was verbally abused and threatened. On two of the occasions he was not allowed to telephone an attorney or his mother. The trial judge directed a verdict for defendants; on appeal the court reversed and ruled that a jury question was presented as to whether the policemen had arbitrarily, unreasonably and without probable cause deprived plaintiff of his constitutional rights (106).

FILING ERRONEOUS CHARGES

When an officer files inapplicable charges against an individual, the policeman may be liable. His fault is gauged by the circumstances. If he knew or should have known that invalid laws were cited, probably he will be responsible.

Plaintiff, a household utensil salesman, was showing a

105. *Nesmith v. Alford,* 318 F. 2d 110 (5th Cir. 1963).
106. *Marland v. Heyse,* 315 F. 2d 312 (10th Cir. 1963).

merchandizing technique to a fellow employee in Illinois. At a downtown sidewalk he gave cards to pedestrians and inquired whether they were interested in home demonstrations. Defendant, policeman, conferred with plaintiff who divulged his name and that he was working but declined further information. When invited to enter the cruiser, plaintiff refused unless arrested. After defendant radioed headquarters for instructions, he arrested plaintiff for soliciting from house to house. Plaintiff was jailed for about two hours before a bondsman arrived. The charge was dismissed. Defendant had been told by his sergeant to bring plaintiff in for soliciting although defendant admitted that he knew this charge to be incorrect. Plaintiff sued defendant for deprivation of his liberty without due process of law. The arrest was without a warrant or probable cause; therefore, plaintiff should recover (107).

As a citizen was driving toward his home in New Mexico, he met plaintiff's truck coming from the opposite direction. The truck swerved, and they almost collided. He turned around and followed the vehicle to obtain its license number. Then he reported the incident, together with his opinion that plaintiff was drunk, to defendant who was a deputy sheriff, constable and village policeman. Defendant pursued the trucker and overtook him outside the village limits. The truck had been swerving. After plaintiff was arrested defendant immediately concluded that plaintiff was not intoxicated and the swerving was caused by the truck's unusual load.

Plaintiff was returned to the village for a hearing before the second defendant, a police magistrate. The latter observed that plaintiff was not drunk and told him so. He was charged with violating an ordinance: driving on the wrong side of the road. Plaintiff pled guilty. He had been detained for about four hours. In an appeal, the prosecutor moved to dismiss charges and refund the fine and court costs. Not only did the village not have an ordinance for driving on the wrong side of the road, but the events took place outside of the village. The arrest may have been legal because it was made by a deputy sheriff; the occurrence happened

107. *Joseph v. Rowlen,* 402 F. 2d 367 (7th Cir. 1968).

within the county, and a violation of state law appeared to have taken place in the deputy's presence. However, the episode in the police court arose from trumped-up charges. Defendants are not immune from liability for compensatory and punitive damages (108).

Two New Jersey state police officers received a message about gunfire in a suburb. They interviewed four or five people who had heard shots near plaintiff's residence. One of the neighbors said that, immediately after a shot, something hit his house. The troopers went to plaintiff's house. They saw two or three spent shotgun shells at the back. Plaintiff admitted getting a gun for his birthday and firing it in the back yard. He and his wife had been drinking.

At the officers' request, he promised not to discharge the weapon again. The policemen left, but several hours later, they were again asked to investigate shooting in the neighborhood. This time they observed six empty cartridges near plaintiff's garage. They saw him and his wife inside their home at a table with a bottle of liquor between them. The troopers were invited in for a drink. When they asked plaintiff about additional gunfire, he replied that he could do anything that he pleased on his own property. He appeared intoxicated and was unable to walk normally. They arrested and jailed him for loitering and creating a disturbance while under the influence of alcohol. After conviction, he appealed successfully on the ground that the charges were inapplicable to his conduct. In a suit for illegal arrest, false imprisonment and malicious prosecution against the officers, the court stated that valid arrests could have been made for attempted voluntary manslaughter; breach of the peace or disorderly conduct. The officers alleged both that they had probable cause to arrest plaintiff and that they acted in good faith. The court held that if these defenses could be proven, the policemen would be exonerated (109).

FAILURE TO TAKE ARRESTEE BEFORE COURT WITHOUT UNDUE DELAY

Generally an officer must present an arrestee to a court without

108. *Vickery v. Dunivan,* 59 N.M. 90, 279 P. 2d 853 (1955).
109. *Anderson v. Haas,* 341 F. 2d 497 (3rd Cir. 1965).

unnecessary delay. Noncompliance subjects a policeman to liability. What constitutes an unreasonable time depends upon the circumstances. Permissible delay may be lengthened by such factors as judicial inaccessibility, other pressing duties of an officer, and the physical or mental condition of the person. Although an individual may waive the right to appear promptly before a court, the waiver must be voluntary.

Defendant, a Vermont constable, arrested plaintiff on a civil writ. He was told that he would be jailed unless he could furnish security for $300. When he was unable to do so, defendant took him to the office of the municipal judge who was absent and then to jail where defendant telephoned another judge. Plaintiff was confined for several hours before his wife paid $135 for his release. He sued defendant for false imprisonment. He had been incarcerated without having first been brought before a magistrate as required by statute. The constable's defense was that he complied with the law by going to one judge's chambers and telephoning another. The court ruled that he had not followed the statutory requirements. Until plaintiff was taken to a judge, he could not be legally jailed. The law must be strictly adhered to; arrest and detention on civil process are drastic measures (110).

Plaintiff was arrested at night in Missouri on a warrant charging him with stealing auto parts and mechanical labor valued at $153.50. Because of unsatisfactory work, he had stopped payment on a check for repairs. Two deputy sheriffs arrested plaintiff at home and took him to jail at about 11:00 p.m. His lawyer and his in-laws arrived promptly to sign a bond. The attorney telephoned a county magistrate who set bond at $1,000. The judge said that the arrestee could either be brought to the judge's home or he would come to the jail to approve the bond. The deputy replied that no bail could be arranged at that late hour. The lawyer requested that the deputy contact the sheriff. When the deputy did, the attorney spoke with the sheriff, who answered that no one got out of jail after five o'clock. Plaintiff was incarcerated until 9:30 a.m. when he was taken before the judge, who had been consulted the previous night, and was freed on bond. Failure to

110. *Thurston v. Leno,* 204 A.2d 106 (Vt. 1964).

release plaintiff earlier constituted false imprisonment (111).

Five hours after an incident occurred in the presence of defendant, Indian policeman, at his home on the Couer d'Alene Indian Reservation, he arrested plaintiff without a warrant for breach of the peace. She was not committing any offense at the time. She was incarcerated for part of a day until she deposited bail. Three days later defendant filed a complaint in a state court. At trial plaintiff was found not guilty. She sued defendant on the grounds of unlawful arrest and detention and also claimed damages for his failure to take her without unnecessary delay to the most accessible magistrate. The arrest was contrary to Idaho statues because plaintiff was not informed of defendant's intention to arrest her, of the cause of arrest or of defendant's authority. Defendant claimed an honest mistake in filing charges in a state court which had no jurisdiction of a crime alleged to have been committed by an Indian on a reservation. However, the court ruled against defendant. He was an experienced Indian policeman and on a previous occasion, under similar circumstances, had brought charges in a state court. They had been dismissed for lack of jurisdiction. The arrest was several hours after a misdemeanor took place in defendant's presence, charges were filed under an inapplicable statute in a court that had no jurisdiction and plaintiff was not brought to a judge without unnecessary delay. Punitive and compensatory damages were awarded to plaintiff (112).

Plaintiff, a resident of Philadelphia, Pennsylvania, was handed a card upon which a statement was written that he was subpoenaed to court as a witness three days later. No subpoena was issued. The appearance date was Yom Kipper, the highest holy day of plaintiff's religion. He was required by his religion to spend from sunrise to sunset in continuous prayer and fasting in the synagogue. He told the parties to the lawsuit of his religious obligations. However, the attorneys in the case demanded a bench warrant from the court for his immediate arrest. Two days thereafter a bench warrant was issued and served on plaintiff at

111. *Librach v. Litzinger,* 401 S.W. 2d 433 (Mo. 1966).
112. *Antelope v. George,* 211 F. Supp. 657 (D. Idaho 1962).

home. After spending six hours incommunicàdo at city hall and not being brought before a judge, he was incarcerated for eight days without presentation to a judge. Plaintiff claimed that the warrant was illegal, and he was imprisoned for contempt without a hearing. He sued the attorneys, court, officials and warden of the county prison. On a hearing of defendants' motion to dismiss, the court ruled that plaintiff had alleged a proper case under the civil rights act (113).

At 5:30 a.m. plaintiff, a 17 year old black, was taken from his home in Chicago by several policemen. They told his parents that they did not believe that he was involved in any crime but was needed for interrogation. They promised to return him in time to attend school that day. At the station plaintiff was questioned about a burglary and fire in an apartment. He denied any knowledge of the matter. During the inquiries he was kicked and hit by an officer. After several hours he was removed to headquarters and required to submit to a polygraph examination. By 11:30 a.m. he was returned to the station. Although his mother was there looking for him, she was not allowed to speak to him. After officers promised food, water and use of the washroom facilities if he confessed, he made three statements. At 4:00 p.m. he was again carried to headquarters and held without charges. The next morning he was arraigned and bound over to the grand jury. He was indicted for murder and burglary and detained without bail for about five months. At the trial, the jury was unable to reach a verdict. Although he was incarcerated for another year, no further action on his case was taken until a nolle prosequi was entered, and he was released.

Plaintiff sued several policemen and the city for deprivation of constitutional rights. His claim was grounded upon being arrested without a warrant, held for 27 hours prior to being brought before a magistrate, not informed of charges, not permitted to use a washroom or receive food and water for 14 hours, not permitted to take bail, not informed of the privilege against self-incrimination and not permitted his right to counsel. Also, he was physically abused to induce a confession, and required to take a lie

---

113. *Johnson v. Crumlish,* 224 F. Supp. 22 (E.D. Pa. 1963).

detector test. On the basis of his confession, he was illegally detained for 18 months. The trial court refused to admit evidence relating to the denial of rights during the 27 hours of detention, and the jury decided for defendants. Upon appeal, the judgment was reversed. The court stated that at a new trial, these matters should be heard; plaintiff has alleged civil rights violations which if proven will result in a verdict in his favor (114).

FALSE IMPRISONMENT AFTER LEGAL DETENTION

The following case is a good example of a situation in which a legal incarceration evolved into an illegal detention. Apparently the arrest and initial imprisonment were justified; however, the validity of the detention ended before the termination of the actual confinement.

Plaintiff was arrested for felony theft by Houston, Texas policemen. Eleven days later at an examining trial he was bound over to the grand jury. Indictments were returned against him for burglary and for theft. Almost two months after his arrest, on motion of the district attorney, the indictments were dismissed. On the following day a list of dismissals, including plaintiff's, was sent to the sheriff's office. The list was not processed. Plaintiff was incarcerated for nine months after the dismissal. His status came to light only after his court appointed attorney attempted to set his case for trial. He sued the sheriff and his surety for false imprisonment. To the defenses that the sheriff acted in good faith and without specific intent to deprive plaintiff of his freedom, the court ruled that the sheriff was liable for the natural consequences of his actions whether or not they were improperly motivated (115).

Good faith is relevant to a false arrest claim because arrests are often made in stressful, urgent situations calling for speed, discretion and on-the-spot evaluation. Thus, privileges apply to officers who in good faith, though by mistake, apprehend persons. But jailers act at their leisure and have an absolute duty to ascertain the authority upon which an inmate is confined. A jailer

114. *Kerr v. City of Chicago,* 424 F. 2d 1134 (7th Cir. 1970).
115. *Whirl v. Kern,* 407 F. 2d 781 (5th Cir. 1969).

cannot lawfully hold a prisoner beyond his sentence. Ignorance by the sheriff of the illegal detention is no excuse.

ARREST AND CONFINEMENT OF PERSON SUSPECTED OF BEING MENTALLY DERANGED

Ordinarily, when there is an urgent need to prevent injury, an officer may arrest and reasonably detain a person who is so insane as to be dangerous to himself or others. This authority is without judicial proceedings or a commitment order. However, a policeman acts at his peril. If the apprehended individual is sane, the arrest and custody are illegal. Some courts absolve an officer if he had probable cause to believe the person to be insane. Whether or not this defense prevails, the elements of urgency and necessity must be established before the arrester is discharged of liability. In many states, statutes cover these circumstances. Officers in these jurisdictions must evaluate the pertinent provisions.

On a sidewalk in San Diego, California, plaintiff displayed a placard protesting denial of his driver's license application. It stated that the governor and department of motor vehicles were crooked, imputed unchastity and wanton sexual activity to a young lady employee of the department and accused government workers of bribes. Several policemen told plaintiff that he had violated the law by carrying the sign without a permit and by exhibiting obscene and indecent literature. He voluntarily went to the station to discuss this with the captain. Then plaintiff was taken to the psychiatric ward where he tried to run away, punched one officer and struggled with others. After plaintiff had been committed to the state hospital without a hearing, he sued the policemen for false imprisonment. California statutes provide that, if a mentally ill person is likely to cause injury to himself or others and requires immediate care or restraint, he may be taken into custody by a policeman who has reasonable cause to believe this is in the person's best interest. The detention took place under this section. The court held that the officers acted properly and were not liable for false imprisonment (116).

---

116. *Whaley v. Kirby,* 208 Cal. App. 2d 232, 25 Cal. Rptr. 50 (1962).

Late at night a man of about 78 years of age came to the police station in Olympia, Washington to complain about a threat on his life. In broken English he related that his son had knocked on his bedroom door and said that he would kill the father. The son allegedly had two guns. The father fled through a window and sought police help. Two officers accompanied him home. The house was dark except for candlelight in the kitchen where the son was sitting and staring straight ahead. He appeared disheveled. When they knocked, he did not respond. They radioed for reinforcements. After repeated demands for the son to open the door, he disappeared into his bedroom and bolted the door. The officers entered the house through the father's open bedroom window. Upon being ordered to throw down any guns he had and open the door, the son replied that he had no gun. He made no further answer and did not open the door. As they broke in, he unfastened the bolt. They seized and handcuffed him and carried him to the station. The apprehension had taken approximately three hours.

He was jailed for about three days before a doctor examined him and pronounced him sane. Then he was released without formal charges ever having been filed. He sued the officers for false imprisonment. They defended on the grounds of a legal arrest: [1] he had threatened his father with a felonious assault and [2] he was mentally unsound and dangerous to be at large. The court ruled for defendants; they had probable cause to arrest the son for either reason (117).

CONCLUSION

Courts do not easily rule that law enforcers are liable for false arrest, false imprisonment and malicious prosecution. Most decisions for plaintiffs are based upon deplorable official behavior. Reasonable conduct is usually a valid defense for a policeman. In arrests, judges give great weight to the urgency and stress of the moment. False imprisonment technically exists after any unlawful apprehension. However, cases illustrate that some detention of an

117. *Plancich v. Williamson,* 57 Wash. 2d 367, 357 P.2d 693 (1960).

illegally arrested individual is permitted if the officer acted in good faith. Malicious prosecution requires the establishment of malice in addition to other elements. Usually a pattern of unauthorized acts must be proven. Concern over these torts should not prevent policemen from fulfilling their duties.

CHAPTER TEN

SEARCH AND SEIZURE

THE Fourth Amendment to the United States Constitution reads as follows:

> The right of the people to be secure in their persons, houses, papers, and effects, against unreasonable searches and seizures, shall not be violated, and no Warrants shall issue, but upon probable cause, supported by Oath or affirmation, and particularly describing the place to be searched, and the persons or things to be seized.

The Fourth Amendment applies to official searches and seizures. It does not apply to searches and seizures by private individuals unless they act under the direction of a law enforcer. Most suits claiming damages for illegal search and seizure revolve around alleged violation of a person's right to be free from unreasonable search and seizure. Basically the defense to such complaints is that the actions were reasonable and authorized by consent, warrant or as incident to arrest.

The fine points of search and seizure, which dictate the admissibility of evidence in criminal proceedings, at times defy the understanding of the best lawyers and judges. In civil litigation courts have adopted more pragmatic guidelines. Ordinarily, policemen can successfully defend contentions of illegal search and seizure by the less stringent standard of reasonable belief rather than probable cause.

Consent to search must be voluntary; it may be limited or revoked at any time. The consenter must not be coerced. In some contexts mere presence of uniformed officers constitutes intimidation. The manner in which permission to search is requested may be so dominating that an individual's will is overcome and voluntariness is negated. In some jurisdictions a person can only consent if he is aware of his right not to do so.

A search warrant which is valid on its face usually will protect officers from civil judgments if they act reasonably. Policemen are expected to heed general law relating to warrants. A daytime warrant cannot be served at any hour; a warrant from one jurisdiction cannot be served in another area; a warrant directed to one group of officers cannot be served by others not included therein; a warrant designating one locality cannot be used elsewhere; a warrant is limited in time and expires thereafter whether or not executed; an executed warrant is no authority for a subsequent search. Local law may modify any of these principles. Usually they prevail and ignoring them subjects an officer to liability.

A legal arrest authorizes a policeman to search the arrestee for weapons and evidence. The legality is the nub of this privilege. The area surrounding the arrestee, which may be searched lawfully, has been diminished by recent court decisions. The exact extent of the search is hotly debated. The crime upon which the arrest is founded also may be relevant to the scope of the search, ranging from minimal in traffic misdemeanors to maximal in armed robberies.

Vehicle search often is not as circumscribed as is that of a dwelling. Open questions remain as to inaccessible areas of cars. Many factors, such as mobility, are involved in automobile searches that are not relevant to houses. Reference to local law will aid in clarifying the legality of vehicle searches.

The words search and seizure are used together so frequently that it is necessary to point out that they represent separate concepts. Just as there may be a search without a seizure there also may be a seizure without a search. Some examples of the latter are seizure of abandoned property or of items in plain view. A search may be illegal even though the seizure is legal because the property is possessed in violation of law. A search may be legal and the seizure illegal when the search is within the area listed on a warrant and goods are removed which are not listed therein and are not evidence of a crime.

REASONABLE CONDUCT

An illegal search does not automatically lead to a civil judgment in favor of the person searched against the officer for violation of constitutional rights. In a Chicago case, two policemen stopped two couples on the street. The officers had probable cause to believe that plaintiff's wife was carrying a concealed weapon in her purse. They found the firearm. Plaintiff attempted to run away but was halted and hastily searched. As the patrolman searched the other couple, his partner made a more thorough search of plaintiff and found a package of heroin in the fly of his trousers. Plaintiff was charged and convicted for unlawful possession of heroin. Upon appeal the conviction was reversed because of illegal search. The court ruled that the first search for weapons was legal; however, the second and more thorough search was unauthorized. In the civil suit, the judge dismissed the complaint on the basis that the officer acted in good faith and with reasonable belief that the search was legal. An indication of the latter is that the search was upheld at the criminal trial; only upon appeal of the conviction was probable cause found to be absent. Policemen on the street will not be compelled to anticipate at their peril such technical evidence rulings when even judges are mistaken on these legal distinctions (118).

Defendants, Massachusetts policemen, observed a pipe on the floor of plaintiff's parked car. Without entering the vehicle, they concluded that the pipe contained a residue of marijuana. A fellow officer, also a defendant, applied for a search warrant based on their report. After a search warrant was issued, the automobile was searched and the pipe taken. Marijuana was in the pipe. In a criminal proceeding against plaintiff, the evidence was suppressed and the case dismissed. Plaintiff sued defendants on the basis that they should have known that probable cause was lacking, in essence a negligence claim. Plaintiff admitted the good faith of defendants in seeking the warrant. A private citizen who sought a warrant under such conditions would not be liable; however, plaintiff contended that officers are bound by a higher standard. The court ruled that, as a policy matter, a policeman should be encouraged to obtain warrants and not be held liable for negligence in doing so. The official who issued the warrant is the

118. *Bowens v. Knazze,* 237 F. Supp. 826 (N.D. Ill. 1965).

protector of the public. If he acts negligently, the policeman is not at fault (119).

UNREASONABLE CONDUCT

Plaintiff, owner and operator of a drive-in theatre in California, sued defendants, sheriff and deputies. During a performance at the drive-in, plaintiff summoned a deputy to arrest a person who had been creating a disturbance. Eight deputies responded, and ordered all patrons out and the theatre closed. As the audience left, the deputies searched each automobile. About three months later fourteen deputies in seven cruisers entered the drive-in, forced occupants out of vehicles and searched the cars. On both occasions some individuals were arrested. No warrants were outstanding for the arrests or searches. Following the two episodes, defendants caused the newspaper publication of prejudicial stories that plaintiff's customers were criminals who engaged in disreputable activities on the premises. Many times after the first occurrence, defendants went into the theatre and patroled with spotlights pointed at the vehicles. These tactics were not used in other local drive-ins. Because of threats of continuing interference with the audience, plaintiff sought an injunction. Defendants argued that an injunction could not prohibit officers from performing their proper duties even though they might behave in an oppressive and unlawful manner or injure plaintiff's business. However, the complaint was that defendants intended to compel plaintiff to change his theatre policies and to interfere with his operation. These purposes are beyond the privileged realm of official duties. Courts may enjoin conduct so motivated (120).

During a nineteen day period, police in Baltimore City, Maryland searched more than three hundred homes, mostly private dwellings, to capture two men believed to have killed one officer and seriously wounded another. In almost every instance the searches were based upon unverified anonymous tips. Arrest warrants were outstanding for the suspects; however, no search warrants were issued. The searches were rationalized on the basis

---

119. *Madison v. Manter,* 441 F. 2d 537 (1st Cir. 1971).

120. *Uptown Enterprises v. Strand,* 15 Cal. Rptr. 486, 195 C. A. 2d 45 (1961).

of probable cause to believe that the persons named in the arrest warrant were at the premises. About fifty or sixty policemen at one period or another were members of a special squad to find the subjects. A police emergency vehicle carrying shotguns, submachine guns, tear gas and bulletproof vests accompanied the men on every search. The procedure followed was to conduct a surveillance with unmarked cars driving by and locating exits, alleyways, etc., but there were no inquiries in the neighborhood about the houses to be searched. No one investigated the tips. Four officers with shotguns or submachine guns knocked on the front doors. Supervisors accompanied them and others surrounded the residences, training weapons on windows and doors.

Several persons, whose homes had been searched, sued the police commissioner to enjoin such practices. Experienced policemen testified that, in serious cases, it was routine procedure to search homes based upon anonymous calls. The court enjoined the police department from searching private homes to arrest any person not known to reside therein, whether with or without an arrest warrant, where the belief that he is located in the house is based only upon an anonymous tip and hence without probable cause (121).

SEARCH OF PERSON: NO CHARGES FILED

One indication that search of a person is illegal is the fact that afterwards no charges are filed. If the officer has probable cause or reasonable belief that the person searched has committed a crime, police procedure dictates an arrest and criminal complaint. Filing improper charges will not legalize an invalid search. However, failure to file charges is a clue to a trooper's awareness that his behavior was unauthorized.

Plaintiffs, husband and wife and children, had retired for the night in their Chicago apartment when thirteen policemen broke in during the early morning. Plaintiffs were routed from bed and forced to stand naked in the living room while officers ransacked every room, emptying drawers and ripping mattress covers. The

121. *Lankford v. Gelston,* 364 F. 2d 197 (4th Cir. 1966).

husband was taken to the police station and detained on open charges for ten hours while he was interrogated about a two-day-old murder. He was not taken to a magistrate though one was accessible nor permitted to call his family or an attorney. No written charges were filed against him. The policemen acted without an arrest or search warrant. The United States Supreme Court ruled that plaintiffs had a valid claim under the civil rights act. They recovered from all thirteen officers (122).

Plaintiff went to Los Angeles International Airport to distribute a religious tract discussing national and international concerns. Also, he intended to protest the arrival of an important Soviet official. As he was walking in a pedestrian crosswalk, he was seized by defendants, city policemen. They took the papers from him, tearing some into pieces and keeping others. They detained him for about ten minutes. Upon release, he demanded the tracts but they refused. They had no warrants and did not tell him that he was under arrest or file charges. Defendants alleged that they were immune because their actions were in accordance with municipal ordinances. The court held that if their conduct deprived plaintiff of federal constitutional rights, it is not a valid defense that the acts were authorized by local enactments (123).

Plaintiff alleged that defendants, five policemen of Los Angeles, California, violated his constitutional rights by four separate acts in public places in the city. Each of the incidents involved a pair of defendants and occurred on Sunset Boulevard or in a nearby restaurant. The episodes ranged from search of plaintiff with intentional blows to his groin in the presence of bystanders to searches without violence and outside the view of others. Defendants acted without arrest, without charges being filed and without bringing plaintiff before a magistrate. Plaintiff can recover if he can establish that the searches and seizures were not made under a legal warrant, incident to arrest or under exceptional circumstances. Searches are arbitrary and unauthorized by law if not conducted to locate articles, which officers have a right to seize, on the person or thing searched (124).

122. *Monroe v. Pape,* 365 U. S. 167, 5 L. Ed. 2d 492, 81 S. Ct. 473 (1963).
123. *Smith v. Cremins,* 308 F. 2d 187, 98 A.L.R. 2d 1154 (9th Cir. 1962).
124. *Cohen v. Norris,* 300 F. 2d 24 (9th Cir. 1962).

At about midnight plaintiff was stopped for running a stop sign by two Texas policemen. After halting, he rolled up the car windows, got out of the vehicle and locked the doors. He was issued a traffic ticket. Although he appeared nervous and agitated, he cooperated and signed the citation. The officers, in continuing their patrol, soon returned to the area where the ticket had been issued. Plaintiff was sitting in his automobile in a parking lot. He was slouched over and relatively motionless. One patrolman approached to find out why plaintiff was there. The policemen observed a large tool box on the rear floorboard. Plaintiff explained that he was reading the ticket, but the light was very poor for reading. The officer asked plaintiff to get out of the vehicle. He abruptly complied, again locking the door. He was arrested, handcuffed and put into the cruiser. They unlocked his automobile and searched the interior and trunk without plaintiff's consent. One of the officers drove the car to the station without plaintiff's permission. The vehicle was again searched. No warrant or consent had been obtained. When nothing to implicate plaintiff was discovered in searches of his person and his automobile, he was freed.

In a civil rights lawsuit, the policemen contended that the arrest was legal and the searches were proper as incident to the arrest. The patrolmen testified that, before arrest, plaintiff had jumped from his car, locked it in an angry manner and suddenly turned on the officer with his hand raised in a threatening gesture. These movements, as part of the grounds for arrest and handcuffing, had not been listed in police reports or the pleadings of this case. Therefore, the court refused to believe that the menacing conduct occurred or, if present, that it was of such a degree as to be a factor in the arrest decision.

The crime for which the arrest was made was never specified; no charges were filed. No probable cause was demonstrated although the officers contended, and the court accepted, that they were following state law and standard police practices. The judgment was that the arrest was unlawful and searches incident thereto were illegal. Even if the apprehension had been correct, the searches were invalid because unreasonable. Good faith attempts to comply with the law, as the officers understood it, is not an acceptable defense under these circumstances. Specific intent to deny plaintiff his constitutional rights was not necessary to a decision for him. The injuries for which he can recover are humiliation, embarassment and discomfort in addition to having his rights trampled upon (125).

LIABILITY OF FEDERAL OFFICERS

The language of the federal civil rights act specifically limits its application to state and local officers; federal agents are not covered. However, the United States Supreme Court recently recognized a right of action against federal officers that is roughly analagous to that against state and local officers under the statute. Federal agents may be held responsible if they violate an individual's constitutional rights. This particular lawsuit was not based upon any statute but arose on a civil complaint alleging humiliation and mental suffering as a result of the agents' unlawful conduct. This decision is a distinct departure from prior cases which universally held that no such remedy was available.

Plaintiff contended that six agents of the Federal Bureau of Narcotics entered his New York apartment and arrested him without a warrant for alleged drug violations. They manacled him in front of his wife and children and threatened to arrest the entire family. Although they had no warrant, they searched the entire dwelling. Plaintiff was taken to the courthouse where he was interrogated, booked and strip searched. He sued the agents, whose names were unknown, for violation of his right to be free from unreasonable searches and seizures. The trial court ordered the complaint served on those federal agents listed in the records of the United States Attorney as the participants in the arrest. Plaintiff is entitled to recover for any injuries he suffered as a result of the agents' violation of the Fourth Amendment. However, as in civil rights act litigation, both good faith and probable cause will be a valid defense for the federal agents. Probable cause in these instances refers to reasonable belief. This is essentially the reasonable man standard of tort law. To prevail the

---

125. *Sexton v. Gibbs,* 327 F. Supp. 134 (D.C. Tex. 1970).

agents must establish that they believed in good faith that their conduct was lawful and that such belief was reasonable (126).

In an opinion that laid some of the groundwork for the rule that federal agents may be liable for violation of constitutional rights, a California court held that federal game wardens were not immune from claims of wrongful seizure of property during search of premises over protest and without a warrant or arrest. Defendants, twelve wardens, appeared at plaintiff's poultry market and seized his records, which he was required by federal law to maintain. Without permission they took wild fowl belonging to plaintiff's customers. The birds not seized were intermingled and left in disarray. Plaintiff demanded return of the property, but this was denied. These officers were authorized to demand production of records or of game in plaintiff's possession. However, the right to inspect did not carry with it the right, without warrant, arrest or consent, to seize property which the wardens inspected (127).

In a different context a federal postal inspector was responsible for several unauthorized acts, including illegal search and seizure. Defendant, United States postal inspector, in investigating the Plymouth, Massachusetts mail robbery, came to plaintiffs' home. The husband was out; the wife was present. To gain admission to the house, defendant falsely told plaintiff wife that he had a warrant to search the premises and an arrest warrant for plaintiff husband. The latter warrant was supposedly based upon a robbery five years before in Ohio. Defendant also said that the husband was suspected in the Plymouth robbery. Defendant restrained the wife from interfering with his entry and search. He seized some currency and two cloth money bags as evidence of the recent crime. The acts of defendant in falsely asserting the existence of a warrant and slandering the husband demonstrated malicious and reckless disregard of plaintiffs' rights (128).

CONCLUSION

When courts evaluate civil claims of illegal search and seizure,

126. *Bivens v. Six Unknown Named Agents of the Fed. Bur. of Narcotics,* 403 U.S. 388, 29 L. Ed. 2d 619, 91 S. Ct. 1999 (1971); on remand 456 F. 2d 1339 (2nd Cir. 1972).
127. *Hughes v. Johnson,* 305 F. 2d 67 (9th Cir. 1962).
128. *Kelley v. Dunne,* 344 F. 2d 129 (1st Cir. 1965).

they balance the public interest in safety of officers and apprehension of criminals with an individual's precious right to be free from official meddling. Judges speak of damages for violation of constitutional rights even though policemen followed local law and department practices, but such cases always turn upon unreasonable conduct. Harrassment beclouds other issues, and courts quickly rectify these tyrannies. When an officer can prove his good faith and reasonable belief in the authority of his acts, he poses an almost impenetrable shield to liability.

CHAPTER ELEVEN

MISCELLANEOUS CONSTITUTIONAL RIGHTS

THIS chapter outlines a variety of lawsuits which assert violations of constitutional rights. Many claims against law enforcers are couched in such terms. For example, false arrest is a deprivation of an individual's right to be free from unreasonable seizure, and battery is punishment without due process of law. However, the courts have not accepted every type of misconduct as proper grounds for constitutional litigation. Ordinarily the complaint must either exclusively be tied to a constitutional provision or allege some form of harrassment before it will be heard in this framework.

Most pleadings in federal courts against state and local officers are filed under the civil rights statute. It was enacted in 1871 as the Ku Klux Klan Act to enforce the due process clause of the Fourteenth Amendment. Congress intended to aid persons deprived of constitutional rights, privileges and immunities by a state official's abuse of his position. The statute had three purposes: first, to override certain kinds of local law; second, to provide a remedy where theoretically adequate state relief was not available in practice, and third, to offer federal jurisdiction supplementary to that of state courts. The 1871 act was virtually unused until the beginning of the 1960's when it was rediscovered in the momentum for civil rights. The Chicago suit (Ch. 10) against the thirteen officers who illegally searched an apartment and falsely arrested the occupant, reached the United States Supreme Court. Times were ripe for such offensive events to be construed under the Ku Klux Klan Act. The highest court, ruling that this sort of oppression constituted a claim under the Act, opened federal tribunals to a flood of litigation.

Some of the general principles that apply to these cases are clear. Others are fashioned each term of court. Municipalities or states cannot be sued; defendants must be individuals. A policeman's misconduct must have been under color of state law. Thus, only official abuses are covered; ordinary citizens are not included. The fact that a law enforcer's behavior was illegal does not make it the act of a private person. Proof of malice or a specific intent to deprive plaintiff of a federal right is unnecessary. Liability flows from the natural consequences of the conduct. Following orders or local laws does not always bar petitioner's recovery; however, in some suits, an officer's honest misunderstanding of law or fact has been a successful answer. The United States Supreme Court has declared that good faith and the existence of probable cause constitute a valid defense.

There are two sections of the civil rights act under which suits against policemen are usually filed. One relates to individual behavior; the second pertains to conspiracies. In order to establish the latter, plaintiffs must prove evil plotting and a resulting overt act.

Although federal officials are not covered by the civil rights act, they may be sued for violation of constitutional rights. The strictures of the act are not binding in these cases, but judges probably will examine the litigation brought under the act to develop appropriate remedies for overreaching by federal agents.

DEPRIVATION OF CONSTITUTIONAL RIGHTS

Both plaintiff's wife and a neighbor telephoned the Massachusetts police for help regarding a disturbance in plaintiff's house. Similar complaints had been made before. Two officers discovered plaintiff and his seventeen-year-old son struggling on the floor. Because the policemen thought that plaintiff was not behaving rationally they carried him (he refused to walk) to a cruiser and took him to the station. After he was searched and his outer garments removed, he was put in a cell. The wife asked the officers to call the family physician. The doctor spoke with plaintiff and then committed him to a mental institution. After confinement of nine or ten days, he was released. He sued the officers, doctor and superintendent of the institution for violation of and conspiracy to violate, his constitutional rights. As to the conspiracy allegation, plaintiff must show deprivation of equal protection of the law or of equal privileges and immunities under the law: invidious discrimination. He failed on this count because he did not establish that he was treated differently than anyone else would have been treated in the same situation. The claim for violation of civil rights was dismissed. The physician was a private citizen and thus not subject to suit under the statute. The superintendent acted in good faith on the basis of a commitment order that was fair and regular on its face. The police were reasonable; they used no more force than necessary. Even if they made a mistake, not every police error amounts to a deprivation of a federally secured right, privilege or immunity (129).

FREEDOM OF SPEECH

Four Navajo youths contended that their First Amendment rights were infringed when they were prevented from distributing leaflets in Gallup, New Mexico, by a policeman, an assistant district attorney and officials of the Inter-Tribal Indian Ceremonial Association. One of the youths wrote a paper entitled "When our Grandfathers Carried Guns" which continued with: "When our Grandfathers Carried Guns, they were free and they were people. If we the Indians of today were like our grandfathers, we would not allow this Ceremonial to be held year after year in this manner and at this place." The leaflet, filled with emotional pronouncements, was highly critical of the Ceremonial and the general treatment of Indians by local people. The paper was first called to defendants' attention when the author was observed handing it out at a crowded entrance to the Gallup Ceremonial. Several Ceremonial officials conferred with the young man. After agreeing to discontinue passing out the leaflet on the grounds, he discussed the situation with a group. One of them was overheard to say that, if the writer so desired, they would tear the place apart or burn it down. Shortly thereafter, they left.

The following day he and others again handed out the leaflet on

129. *Joyce v. Ferrazzi,* 323 F. 2d 931 (1st Cir. 1963).

the grounds. The officials and a policeman sought the advice of an assistant district attorney who interpreted the paper as a *call to arms.* He stated that stopping distribution was necessary to prevent a riot. The Indians were told that, if they continued their activities, they would be arrested. They left, and no arrests occurred. No attempts were made to halt circulation except on the grounds near the grandstands. Wide publication took place throughout the city, particularly along a parade route.

The court held that the state has the power to protect and preserve its property for the use to which it was dedicated. There is no constitutional right to hand out pamphlets anywhere and everywhere. Defendant's actions were reasonable to avoid a disastrous situation which they in good faith believed could happen. There was a clear and present danger of violence; defendants were not required to wait to take preventive measures until the feared conditions erupted. Freedom of speech does not sanction incitement to riot (130).

A corporation sought to permanently enjoin the police commissioner and commander of the morals squad of Philadelphia, Pennsylvania from seizing allegedly obscene material without a prior judicial determination of obscenity. The corporation operated a store that sold incense, candles, jewelry, buttons and posters. The wares were exhibited in a window. Children, aged 4 to 12 years, passed by going to and coming from two nearby elementary schools. A morals squad agent purchased two buttons which had been on display. Immediately following the sale, other policemen, with a search warrant, seized several hundred buttons and arrested three employees. Before the warrants were issued and the arrests made, there had been no court finding as to the obscenity of the seized articles. The employees were held not guilty of possession of obscene material.

A month later, police armed with search warrants raided the shop, seized a number of posters and apprehended several employees. Before their trial, a third raid was conducted. Objects, similar to those taken earlier, were seized. Employees were arrested for possession of obscene materials and corrupting the

130. *Benson v. Rich,* 448 F. 2d 1371 (10th Cir. 1971).

morals of a minor. None of the arrestees on the second or third raids were convicted. No judicial rulings of obscenity were made before any of the raids. Each time the commander of the morals squad determined what constituted obscenity. He based his conclusion on the fact that children looked at the merchandise: slogans about sex and photos of nudes. Defendants did not try to learn why the arrestees were not convicted or consult attorneys for advice.

Although obscenity is not protected by the First Amendment, the Fourteenth Amendment requires that states conform to due process standards in their regulation of obscenity. Procedures must insure against the curtailment of constitutionally protected expression. It was held that plaintiff was entitled to have an adversary hearing upon the obscenity of the materials before the police could seize them even pursuant to a warrant. An injunction was issued to prohibit the morals squad commander from illegally seizing any allegedly obscene article from plaintiff. The police commissioner was directed to prevent any officers under his command from so doing (131).

FREEDOM OF THE PRESS

A group of news photographers brought a class action against the City of Chicago, the police superintendent and certain officers whose names were unknown, for a permanent injunction prohibiting interference with the constitutional right to gather and report news. Plaintiffs also requested the superintendent to take appropriate measures, including orders, rules and regulations, to guarantee cessation of force and intimidation against them. The complaint was filed during mid-week of the 1968 Democratic National Convention. Defendants' motion to dismiss was denied on the grounds that plaintiffs had stated a valid civil rights claim. Injunctive relief is available when government officials have notice of unconstitutional acts of their subordinates and fail to prevent recurrence of such behavior. It does not matter whether the abuse is actively encouraged and directed by the supervisors or merely

---

131. *Leslie Tobin Imports, Inc. v. Rizzo,* 305 F. Supp. 1135 (E.D. Pa. 1969).

acquiesced in by them. If the alleged misconduct is established at trial, some form of relief will be ordered (132).

A newspaper publisher in Dayton, Ohio sued police and other municipal officers of the city for deprivation of civil rights. Defendants refused to permit plaintiff's reporter to be on the public streets in the vicinity of a fire. He was forceably removed from the streets, while other newsmen were allowed to remain. The trial judge dismissed the complaint, but the appellate court reversed on the grounds that a violation of civil rights had been stated. At a hearing, defendants may prove that they exercised their authority to restrict the use of the streets for reasons of public safety, and that the reporter deserved the treatment accorded him because he failed to obey proper police orders (133).

CRUELTY

Plaintiff alleged violation of United States Constitutional Amendments Four, Six, Eight and Fourteen by officers of Houston, Texas. Early one evening an individual shot both plaintiff and a policeman. When two other officers arrived on the scene, they concluded without any inquiry that plaintiff had shot the policeman. They struck plaintiff on the head with a club, handcuffed him with hands behind his back, and continued to hit him on the head and shoulders before throwing him into a closed van. Once inside, they beat and kicked him in the neck, face and head, breaking the bones in his face and knocking out several teeth. No charges were filed against plaintiff, and he was released. The count for conspiracy, naming the chief as co-conspirator, was dismissed because it was not supported by any factual assertions. The lower court dismissed the claims of deprivation of constitutional rights on the grounds that plaintiff must first sue in state tribunals before bringing a complaint under federal law. On appeal, the latter ruling was reversed. Federal relief may be sought before pursuing state remedies (134).

132. *Schnell v. City of Chicago,* 407 F. 2d 1084 (7th Cir. 1969).
133. *Dayton Newspapers, Inc. v. Starick,* 345 F. 2d 677 (6th Cir. 1965).
134. *Burnett v. Short,* 441 F. 2d 405 (5th Cir. 1971).

SELF-INCRIMINATION

Plaintiff sued three Baltimore City, Maryland policemen under the civil rights act for obtaining an incriminating statement from him without advising him of his constitutional right to remain silent. He was accosted by defendants on a public street. They were accompanied by a woman who accused him of assaulting and robbing her a few minutes earlier. They interrogated him without informing him of the *Miranda* rights. He made a statement that he would not have made if so advised. At the police station he was again questioned without being told his rights. At criminal trial, his answers were read into evidence. He was convicted and was serving a five year sentence. Defendants filed a motion to dismiss on the grounds that the complaint failed to state a claim upon which relief can be granted. The case was dismissed. *Miranda* does not make an interrogation which violates its precepts into an actionable tort. An improper interrogation is not itself a tort. Nor does an interrogation, in and of itself, amount to a denial of the constitutional rights of the person being interrogated (135).

RIGHT TO COUNSEL

Plaintiff, a prisoner of the state of California, was convicted of mayhem and assault with a deadly weapon. He alleged a valid claim of violation of his constitutional right to counsel under the Sixth Amendment, against the police chief of Millbrae, California. Before plaintiff surrendered to the chief, the latter had been told by plaintiff's attorney that he would instruct his client not to make any statement. Nevertheless, the chief questioned plaintiff without telling him of his lawyer's orders not to talk or advising him of his rights. The chief also disregarded plaintiff's request for his attorney. Plaintiff contended that he did not confess, that the chief altered the electronic tapes of the interrogation to make it appear that plaintiff had incriminated himself. A week before the chief's asserted acts, the United States Supreme Court handed

---

135. *Allen v. Eicher,* 295 F. Supp. 1184 (D.C. Md. 1969).

down the *Escobedo* opinion on the right to counsel and inadmissibility of statements when police violate this right. Both *Escobedo* and the instant situation dealt with the Sixth Amendment. In plaintiff's criminal trial the question of violation of this provision was not decided because the court, counsel and prosecutor agreed not to introduce the evidence. The defense that plaintiff's conviction bars this civil rights suit is erroneous. Information derived from the constitutionally defective procedure was used; therefore, the conviction itself cannot preclude this litigation (136).

RACIAL DISCRIMINATION

Plaintiff, a black musician and part-time college student, sued the mayor, councilmen, police chief and four policemen of a village in Minnesota for racial discrimination in repeatedly stopping him for traffic violations and conspiring to deprive him of his civil rights. The village contained many well-to-do homes, and most of its inhabitants were Caucasian. It bordered, on the east and north, a section of Minneapolis which was rather heavily populated with blacks. Police records for a period of more than a year revealed that approximately 21 per cent of all arrests in the village were of blacks and one-half of these arrests were made by three of the defendants. For nine months plaintiff had played in a band at a club situated near the center of the village. During that period the local police had repeatedly stopped his vehicle without proper justification. Four times he had been issued tickets, and on one occasion had been incarcerated briefly and his car towed away. Plaintiff offered no substantial proof as to how defendants treated whites or that they were treated differently than blacks. But the court stressed that the jurors were entitled to adopt a standard of reasonableness based upon their own common experiences and ordinary good sense. Unfair treatment of other blacks was shown. Defendants gave their version of these incidents. The jury considered the contradictory testimony and decided against the chief and three officers. Since this was a

136. *Ney v. Calif.*, 439 F. 2d 1285 (9th Cir. 1971).

proper question for jury evaluation, and there was evidence to support the verdict, it was affirmed on appeal (137).

HARRASSMENT

A class of persons sued the police commissioner and certain park officials of Philadelphia, Pennsylvania for unconstitutional arrests, interrogation and interference with their freedom of association, assembly and speech. The class was described in the complaint as individuals who are unconventional (or are so regarded by defendants) in appearance, manner and life style, as compared with the mainstream of society. One summer night Philadelphia police raided a city park and arrested 27 youths, including two of the plaintiffs. They were taken to the station, photographed and interrogated. The questions related to alleged criminal conduct in only a general way. After about an hour of custody, they were freed. No charges were lodged and the photographs remained on file. Three weeks later at another raid on the park, 20 youths were apprehended, including one plaintiff. The same processes occurred. At various times during this period young persons were temporarily detained by park guards, carried to the guard house, searched, interrogated and warned to stop frequenting the park. Several of them were threatened with physical violence if they did not leave the park. Some guards discriminated against plaintiffs in enforcing park regulations.

It was found that there was no probable cause to believe that the arrestees were guilty of any crimes. It is not an offense to be a *hippie.* The police cannot arrest on the basis of suspicion, or even probable cause to believe that an individual is a homosexual or narcotics addict. Penal laws are directed toward actions, not status. It may be a crime to possess narcotics or engage in homosexual acts; however, mass arrests without investigation go far beyond permissible limits of police authority. The real motive for the arrests and discrimination was to rid the park of hippies. Although not admitting anything, defendants agreed to cease, and in fact did cease the offensive conduct; therefore, an injunction

137. *Lyle v. Teresi,* 327 F. Supp. 683 (D. C. Minn. 1971).

was not necessary. Courts are not equipped to supervise day-to-day operations of officers. However, jurisdiction of this matter was retained so that appropriate relief could be granted should the need arise. Records derived from the two mass arrests were ordered expunged and all photographs returned or destroyed (138).

CONCLUSION

Constitutional protections envelop most officer-citizen clashes. More than anyone else, policemen have the authority to limit an individual's liberty. Overbearing enforcement of this power has led to judgments against law enforcers. Examination of the cases demonstrates that policemen will get their day in court. A favorable verdict will result if officers can establish the reasonableness and necessity of their conduct.

138. *Hughes v. Rizzo,* 282 F. Supp. 881 (E.D. Pa. 1968).

CHAPTER TWELVE

RIGHT TO PRIVACY

EVERYONE has a right to be let alone. The extent of this privacy depends upon the public status of the individual, the waiver of the right in a particular instance and the benefit to society in discovering and disseminating specific information. From a weighing of personal and public interests emerges the balance between invasion of privacy and acceptable investigation.

In most states protection of privacy is based on the common law. Some statutes spell out the remedy: generally with a focus on use without consent of a person's name or photograph for commerical purposes. Laws which limit wiretapping and distribution of credit information set guidelines which may be referred to in asserted invasions of privacy. Conviction of a crime under such statutes will not bar civil suits by injured parties.

Invasion of privacy closely resembles defamation of character and intentional infliction of emotional distress. However, defamation, as discussed in detail in Chapter 13, involves damage to reputation in the community; invasion of privacy is harm to one's own feelings. Intentional infliction of emotional distress requires proof of a deliberate and malicious campaign of harassment or intimidation which is not necessary to privacy complaints. Also, in many jurisdictions, such emotional injury without physical damage is not recognized as a legal cause of action.

As in most torts, right of privacy is evaluated by a reasonable man standard and not by the sensitivities of the thin-skinned. Some exposure of one's private sphere is inevitable in a crowded civilization. Only unreasonable and serious interference with someone's desire not to have his affairs made known to others, or his likeness exhibited, results in liability. Policemen and private investigators ordinarily are adjudged to be serving society in collecting and disseminating information. When their activities exceed public need and harm an individual, courts will enjoin and penalize them.

DISCOVERY OF FACTS

One of the major functions of a private investigator is to discover facts. Insurance companies employ his skills to ferret out fictitious or exaggerated claims. Two recent trials involved such techniques. A Georgia plaintiff was hurt in an automobile collision and sued the driver of the other vehicle. The latter's insurance company hired defendant detective agency to determine the extent of plaintiff's injuries. Over a period of four months the sleuths slunk around her house near the windows, cut a hole in the hedge to spy into the windows, parked close to her home from early morning until late at night, followed her on the streets, into stores and public places, repeatedly drove past her house, and came to her door pretending to have business with her. On one occasion, she returned home at night and was so closely followed that she ran into the house in panic, hit a piece of furniture and was knocked unconscious. Her neighbors noticed the surveillance and stopped associating with her. The court acknowledged that plaintiff had waived part of her right of privacy by filing a lawsuit; however, plaintiff won the case because the surveillance went beyond reasonable and unobstrusive observation (139).

A Pennsylvania private detective fared better in court. Petitioner was hurt in an automobile accident and made a claim against the other driver. The latter's insurance company retained detectives to discover whether claimant could freely move her limbs. On one day, from 8:00 a.m. to 5:30 p.m., the investigators watched claimant's neighborhood. While driving in traffic, she noticed the detectives following her and holding a camera. The court said that the investigation was reasonable. All of the shadowing took place in the open on public thoroughfares where the events could be seen by passers-by. There was no trespassing on her property or spying in her windows. Motion pictures of her

139. *Pinkerton Nat'l. Det. Agn., Inc. v. Stevens,* 108 Ga. App. 159, 132 S.E. 2d 119 (1963).

movements were an acceptable means of securing evidence for trial. No charge was made that the photographs would be exhibited publicly. Plaintiff surrendered a portion of her seclusion by filing a claim for personal injuries; some inquiry must be expected to expose fabricated claims (140).

OVERZEALOUS SURVEILLANCE

A notorious case was brought in New York by consumer champion Ralph Nader against General Motors Corporation. Wiretapping, eavesdropping and overzealous surveillance by defendant constituted invasion of privacy. Defendant's employee followed Nader into a bank and got close enough to him to observe the denominations of the bills withdrawn from his account. Merely watching a person in a public place is not a violation, but one does not automatically make public everything he does in a public place. The court found no invasion of privacy in the charge that defendant paid girls to accost Nader with illicit proposals or to telephone him repeatedly at odd hours. If intent is established, such acts may add up to intentional infliction of emotional distress. Character disparagement by the General Motors employee during interviews of Nader's acquaintances might amount to defamation, but the information gleaned about him was already known to others and could hardly be regarded as private to him. Nonetheless, the decision on the pleadings added some broad interpretations to this legal remedy which will aid future plaintiffs (141).

In Georgia, Ford Motor Company was sued for trespass, illegal seizure and invasion of privacy based upon breaking into petitioner's home to recover articles allegedly belonging to Ford. An employee of Ford, together with several policemen, drove into plaintiff's yard in three marked units and a paddy wagon, and while no one was at home, forced open a window, entered and removed new Ford automobile parts. The property belonged to plaintiff and was returned to him the next day. Upon these facts, the court ruled that defendant, through its agent, had invaded

140. *Forster v. Manchester,* 410 Pa. 192, 189 A. 2d 147 (1963).

141. *Nader v. General Motors Corp.,* 25 N.Y.S. 2d 560, 255 N.E. 2d 765 (1970).

plaintiff's privacy whether or not any one was present at the time (142).

RETENTION OF RECORDS

Cases similar to those listed above have been initated against policemen, but the thrust of recent litigation lies in challenging surveillance of dissenters and handling of official records. A further step that courts may be expected to take is prohibiting transmittal of records that do not contain dispositions of charges. Thus far plaintiffs have been rather unsuccessful in civil suits which contest gathering of information. Appearance in public places generally waives right of privacy, and photographing ordinarily has been permitted. The chilling effect on First Amendment freedoms by these pictures is of less weight than the social utility of this law enforcement practice. However, the *Nader* position of invasion of privacy by overzealous surveillance undoubtedly will prevail in a future case, if police push accepted techniques under aggravated circumstances.

Suits to expunge arrest records of persons acquitted of crimes are being won on the theory of invasion of privacy. Weight is added to these claims by analogy to new legislation clearing the slates of those convicted of minor drug offenses and of juvenile violators. Federal law and many state statutes give judges the discretion to seal arrest and first offense conviction records of drug possessors. Juvenile codes spell out protections for youngsters, such as strict limitations on fingerprinting and photographing and special handling of records to avoid prying eyes.

A California case stated the viewpoint of most courts in the past on the dissemination of police reports. Plaintiff charged improper distribution of erroneous information contained in his police records. He had been arrested and on probation as a juvenile for grand theft auto. From a police photograph sent upon request to another department, he had been identified as the passer of a forged check. This identification and a notation of the four aliases

---

142. *Ford Motor Co. v. Williams,* 108 Ga. App. 21, 132 S.E. 2d 206 (1963).

used on the fictitious checks, was noted on his rap sheet. No complaint had been filed against plaintiff for forgery because he was out of state. With all of this data, the record had been sent, upon request, to other police departments. Plaintiff believed that the listings were incorrect and asked to examine his file. When he saw the rap sheet, he protested certain errors. Plaintiff was told that maintenance of the records was required by statute unless the agency which had submitted the data stated that it was wrong. Plaintiff sued for damages instead of petitioning that agency to correct the information. The court upheld the police conditional privilege to publish the material to law enforcement organizations upon request and pursuant to law (143).

Another tack taken in a case seeking expunction of police records was to enjoin their distribution except to certain law enforcement officials and to those government agencies to which plaintiff applied for a job. The suit sought to compel the United States Attorney General and the Director of the F.B.I. to remove plaintiff's fingerprints and a reference to his detention by California police from the F.B.I.'s criminal identification files. An arrest for burglary was listed without a statement that there was no prosecution. Plaintiff had complained that the information was misleading and incomplete. He anticipated harm from its publication to law enforcement agencies, potential employers and others (144).

The trend moves toward upholding an acquitted individual's demand for expunction of arrest records. In the early 1900's courts in Louisiana (145) and Maryland (146) prohibited policemen from including photographs in a rogue's gallery of those who had not been convicted of a crime. Barring public display of an innocent person's photograph was an exception to the general rule that the handling of arrest data was within the realm of police discretion. Much later, courts recognized the right of an illegally arrested person to have records cancelled. Complaints of this type have been filed in connection with dragnet arrests or arrests made

143. *White v. State of Calif.*, 17 Cal. App. 3d 621, 95 Cal. Rptr. 175 (1971).
144. *Menard v. Mitchell,* 430 F. 2d 486 (D.C. Cir. 1970).
145. *Itzkovitch v. Whitaker,* 115 La. 479, 39 So. 499 (1905).
146. *Downs v. Swan,* 111 Md. 53, 73 A. 653 (1909).

for purposes other than prosecution, such as for harassment or intimidation to discourage voting registration.

Several recent cases have compared the interest of the government in retaining arrest records with the detriment to the individual and ruled against the state. Many factors besides guilt, such as technical defenses of lack of speedy trial or illegal search, determine the outcome of a criminal trial. Therefore, basing the handling of arrest records only on the result of a prosecution is unwarranted. A preferable system would be to weigh each situation according to objective standards, with the court as the final arbiter. Recent decisions illustrate the views of some judges on this question.

When charged with refusing to be inducted into the Army, defendant contended that his attorney had advised him not to step forward at the swearing in because he soon would receive a deferment. The United States Attorney insisted that he be arrested, fingerprinted and photographed. Within one-half hour of this process, plaintiff voluntarily was sworn in. The complaint was dismissed without conviction. The government contested his motion to expunge and destroy the photograph and fingerprints on the grounds that no statute prescribed this and that the same information was available from the Army. The judge held that a criminal identification, when no charges are pending and there has been no conviction, constitutes an unwarranted attack upon an individual's character and reputation and violates his right of privacy. The court ordered destruction of these records, forbade their transmittal to any other government, government agency or any person and decreed that the United States Attorney General promptly notify the court of the time, place and manner in which the records had been destroyed (147).

A Washington court took a similar position in a trial for assault. After the charges were dismissed, the accused demanded the return of her fingerprints and photographs. The police argued that the statutory duty to take fingerprints and photographs implied an authority to retain them in the absence of a law directing otherwise. Two assumptions which have favored retention of

147. *U.S. v. Kalish,* 271 F. Supp. 968 (D.P.R. 1967).

arrest records are that 1) the arrestee is guilty and 2) his violation indicates that he may commit more crimes. An acquittal apparently negates both premises. Therefore, the right of privacy of an individual, who has been acquitted and as to whom no further basis remains for retention of identification data, must be compared with the public need for this information. Before the state can prevail, it must show a compelling necessity. The fact that no statute provided such procedure was held to be a constitutionally defective omission in the law and delivery to the accused was ordered (148).

Legislation in some states provides for the returning of photographs and fingerprints to a person who is acquitted. Such enactments probably will become commonplace in the 1970's.

A tricky question that may emerge in future litigation is how long may police keep arrest records. What effect will lapse of time have on the retaining of photographs and fingerprints of those convicted of minor offenses or of persons not prosecuted due to technicalities? A California case ruled on lapse of time under dissimilar facts; the decision is useful by analogy. A magazine published an article containing plaintiff's name and some facts about, but not the date of, a hijacking offense that he had committed some years before. After the crime, he had developed a law abiding reputation among people who were unaware of his past. Plaintiff sued the magazine for invasion of privacy and won (149).

Other courts have held to the contrary. Once a person is newsworthy no period of time changes his status: in effect privacy is waived. Future decisions probably will examine the legitimate purpose of the publication and then balance public versus private interests. Similar considerations may determine questions regarding retention and dissemination of law enforcement records. New federal laws prohibit distribution of arrest information to employers and credit sources. Further enactments may bar fingerprinting or photographing in minor crimes or erect barriers to publication of data on offenders after a period of time.

---

148. *Eddy v. Moore,* 5 Wash. App. 334, 487 P.2d 211 (1971).
149. *Briscoe v. Reader's Digest Ass'n.,* 93 Cal. Rptr. 866, 483 P.2d 34 (1971).

NOTORIETY

Victims of some crimes seek to keep their names from being publicized. The situation that comes to mind is rape. Statutes prohibiting publication of the identity of victims of sex crimes have been held constitutional. Of course, the defendant must be given adequate information to permit preparation of his defense. But limiting dissemination of the names of these victims benefits the public by encouraging the reporting of rapes. Other offenses to which this rationale may apply are burglaries. Many householders fear that notice that their premises have been broken into may be an invitation to others. Newspaper columns of the police blotter type list this data. When such complaints are filed, courts will weigh freedom of the press against invasion of privacy. With the nationwide concern about increased burglaries, the individual's claims probably will prevail.

ABUSE OF INFORMATION

Plaintiff went to the Chino, California police department to file charges for an assault upon her. A policeman told her that, in connection with her complaint, she would have to be photographed. He took her to a room in the station, locked the door and directed her to undress. She objected that this was unnecessary because her bruises would not show up. She protested both the taking of photographs of her in the nude and the indecent positions which he ordered her to assume. However, she relented, and the pictures were taken. A policewoman was present in the station, but she was not requested to be present and was not there during the photographing. Later that month the officer told plaintiff that the pictures did not come out and that he had destroyed them. Instead, he circulated them among the department personnel. A year and a half later two other policemen made additional prints and also distributed them among the employees. Several months afterwards, plaintiff discovered that the original photos had not been destroyed and that additional prints had been made. The court ruled that all three officers had arbitrarily intruded upon plaintiff's privacy. In its decision the court relied upon the lack of necessity for the pictures which were taken over plaintiff's protests, the failure to summon an available female officer during the photographing and the unwarranted circulation among the police personnel (150).

PRISONERS' RIGHTS

Prisoners are demanding right of privacy in their communications. Conferences with attorneys are probably covered by the Sixth Amendment (right to counsel), and contacts with the media come under the First Amendment (freedom of the press). Two cases explored prisoners' rights of privacy in conversations with relatives and other convicts. Both decisions denied a right of privacy in these situations under the theory that lack of privacy was an adjunct to imprisonment. In one of these suits a tape recording was made of conversations between persons in adjoining cells (151). The other incident involved a visit between a prisoner and his sister, which had been recorded by a device attached to the jail's intercom system (152). Recent litigation has limited censorship by mail and has expanded visitation and correspondence privileges. Right of privacy is moving into prisons; the goal of incarceration now emphasizes rehabilitation.

CONCLUSION

Right of privacy litigation is a fairly new area of concern to private detectives and policemen. An increase in these lawsuits is predictable because of plaintiffs' successes in recent cases, a growing public awareness of legislation limiting information dissemination by government agencies and businesses, and a distaste for obtrusive surveillance. The social value of investigations and police record retention will be scrutinized; only compelling public need will justify their continuance in the future.

---

150. *York,v. Story,* 324 F. 2d 450 (9th Cir. 1963).
151. *Peo. v. Ross,* 236 Cal. App. 2d 364, 46 Cal. Rptr. 41 (1965).
152. *Peo. v. Morgan,* 197 Cal. App. 2d 90, 16 Cal. Rptr. 838 (1961).

CHAPTER THIRTEEN

DEFAMATION OF CHARACTER

THE two forms of the tort of defamation of character are libel and slander. The basis for a libel suit is a derogatory written statement which harms an individual's reputation. Slander is the same type of injury arising from speech. Communication of the remarks by defendant to a third party, usually referred to as publication, is an element of libel and slander. Plaintiffs win verdicts by proving unauthorized publication, malice or negligence in gathering data. However, a number of defenses are available to officers and departments.

A defamatory statement is not one that is simply unfavorable to a person. The communication must expose him to hatred, ridicule or contempt, or say that he has been involved in an activity that tarnishes the community opinion of him. These are necessarily vague categories because libel and slander relate to the standards of society. Whether or not an allegation is defamatory depends upon shifting mores and the comprehension of the reader or listener that the remark is shameful. For example, in the past few years the term *pig* for a policeman has become less odious and the term *boy* for a black more humiliating. *Pig* has been neutralized by policemen through adopting it as a symbol for pride, integrity and guts. *Boy* has become synonymous with racism and emasculation.

Defamatory words directed toward a large group are not grounds for a lawsuit unless the petitioner proves that they relate specifically to him. An officer's jibe that "all lawyers are shysters" is too broad an attack in a community with one hundred or more attorneys unless additional references point at a particular lawyer. As the size of the defamed group shrinks and the censure defines one member, plaintiff's case improves.

Generally a libel complainant may win whether or not he demonstrates specific monetary injury; slander suits are dismissible without such proof. Exceptions to this requirement of establishing actual damages for slander are: 1) imputation of a crime, of a loathesome disease or unchastity of a woman; or 2) accusations that affect plaintiff in his occupation. Proof of such slander or of any libel will give the defamed person a right to at least nominal damages. The jury, or judge if the trial is nonjury, then estimates the amount of recovery. Depending upon the offensiveness of the statement and personal disgrace, the award may be either slight or substantial.

Although libel and slander usually refer to words, other types of expression are defamatory: cartoons, photographs, gestures or conduct which ridicules plaintiff. The legal classification of libel or slander is determined by whether or not the communication is embodied in a permanent form. For example, a photograph would be libelous and a gesture slanderous. If police conspicuously follow a reputable dentist for a considerable time, he may have been slandered. Exhibiting movies of the surveillance might be libelous.

Police in a small New Mexico town, upon routinely checking a license through N.C.I.C., were informed that the vehicle in question was stolen and in the hands of an armed and dangerous robbery suspect. Confirmation was sought and received. They followed the car to a small dwelling. Several officers converged on the home and watched the exits. The police on the porch unholstered their weapons and knocked on the door. A frightened lady explained that she had just bought the car and was unaware of its history. Further verification of the N.C.I.C. report revealed that it was incorrect. Although the officers apologized and explained their mistake, the woman sued them for harm to her reputation among neighbors who saw the incident. After the filing of preliminary pleadings and a refusal by the officers to settle out of court, she dismissed the case.

DEFENSES

Truth is an affirmative defense to libel and slander which must be pleaded and proven. It is essential to show that the defamatory material is completely true, not just partially correct. If defendant cannot prove truth, he has reiterated the defamation in his answer to the complaint and plaintiff may receive additional damages.

Another defense to defamation is privilege; thus, the issuer is immune from liability. A privileged utterance is one that, except for the occasion on which or the circumstances under which it is made, would be grounds for a defamation suit. If absolute privilege exists, there is no liability even though defendant acted with malice. Consent to defamation gives complete immunity. Absolute privilege applies to court pleadings and testimony. This immunity is broadly interpreted; however, it does not cover obvious irrelevancies.

One type of privilege is that involved in a court proceeding, as illustrated by a recent incident. After a high speed pursuit from an interstate highway through a residential area, a trooper in New Mexico stopped a motorist. Sixteen traffic citations were issued for reckless driving, running a stop sign and speeding up to 100 m.p.h. in an 80 m.p.h. zone to 90 m.p.h. in a 25 m.p.h. zone. In the blanks on the forms for occupation the officer wrote: "gay-blade," "gay-blade thief" and "auto thief." Although the uniform traffic citation is a court complaint for violations of the state motor vehicle code, these listings on the citations are libelous as unnecessary and derisive. The driver would win at least nominal recovery because no privilege exists for name calling on a traffic citation; punitive damages probably would flow from the malice.

The other type of privilege is referred to as qualified or conditional. This is the form that usually applies to policemen in the discharge of their duties. Malice defeats a qualified privilege; good faith and reasonableness are necessary.

Transmission among officers or conversations between policemen and a defamed person ordinarily do not amount to libel or slander because no third party is involved. Even if there is publication, responsibility may be denied if the remark was within the scope of law enforcement duties and was made without malice.

A sheriff was sued for slander for telling his deputy that plaintiff was violating the liquor laws. The deputy applied for a search warrant on this information. A Kentucky court ruled the communication to be absolutely privileged as in the discharge of official duties (153). A New York court held it to be a qualified privilege when an officer informed a landlord that his tenants were running an illegal disorderly house. The conversation resulted from a request by the officer to pass through the premises. No proof was in the record that the policeman knew the information to be false or that the exchange with the landlord was carelessly spoken within the hearing of others or was in stronger language than was justified (154).

A West Virginia court found actual malice in a policeman's statement and decided that he had exceeded a qualified privilege. While the officer was inspecting city parking meters, he accused a merchant of breaking the meter outside his business by jamming a slug in it. The wrongdoing was loudly declared in the presence of third persons (155).

A privilege exists for derogatory remarks in reference to hiring or discharge of employees if the declaration is in the general line of an officer's duty. However, public explanations of the reasons for firing of deputies has been held unprivileged and thus slanderous. A District of Columbia court ruled that a United States marshal had a duty to investigate complaints against his deputies but that he had no obligation to disclose the matter to the public (156). In a Pennsylvania case, an individual asked why the town marshal had not employed a certain applicant. The marshal answered that he had heard that the applicant was a church robber. This statement of the basis for not hiring was held to be privileged (157).

In Pennsylvania, charges by a police captain to a civil service commission against an officer resulting in his loss of pay and suspension were absolutely privileged. The accusations were brought to a proper tribunal by an authorized person (158). In a Virginia police disciplinary case, the court extended a qualified privilege to defamatory remarks made in connection with an administrative proceeding. The court did, however, give plaintiff

153. *Catron v. Jasper,* 303 Ky. 598, 198 S.W. 2d 322 (1946).
154. *Morton v. Knipe,* 128 App. Div. 94, 112 N.Y.S. 451 (1908).
155. *City of Mullens v. Davidson,* 57 S.E. 2d 1, 13 A.L.R. 2d 887 (W. Va. 1949).
156. *Colpoys v. Gates,* 73 App. D.C. 193, 118 F. 2d 16 (1941).
157. *Brockerman v. Keyser,* 1 Phila. 243, 5 Clark 151 (Pa. 1851).
158. *Krouse v. Driscoll,* 78 Pa. D. & C. 72 (Pa. 1951).

an opportunity to prove defendant's actual malice in order to defeat the privilege (159).

Over the past several years judges have carved out a significant defense to suits brought by public officials: fair criticism of those in the spotlight. The rationale is that public concern and freedom of expression under the First Amendment confer a liberty to speak about public matters. The defense is limited to fair comment relating to matters of public interest. It extends to false allegations of fact except where actual malice is demonstrated. Fair comment will surely be asserted in cases arising from criticism by officers of their supervisors.

CONCLUSION

Libel consists of unprivileged defamatory writings. Derogatory speech may amount to slander. Any defamation must be published to a third party to be tortious. Absolute privilege is a defense to claims of libel and slander. Malice, if proven, will override a qualified privilege. While in some jurisdictions officers have an absolute privilege for communications made within the scope of their duty, generally policemen have only a conditional privilege.

159. *Elder v. Holland,* 208 Va. 15, 155 S. E. 2d 369 (1967).

CHAPTER FOURTEEN

FAILURE TO ACT

POLICEMEN have a positive duty to maintain the peace and enforce the law. If they do not perform, they are derelict in their duty. In legal terminology, this amounts to nonfeasance. A consequence of this failure to act may be disciplinary proceedings by an employer. Ordinarily, persons hurt by violators who were not apprehended by a patrolman do not win judgments against him. The general rule is that police protection is owed to the public; not to any particular individual. Therefore, failure of an officer to enforce the law is not grounds for a successful suit against him by an injured citizen.

A decision by an Arizona court illustrates this principle. A deputy sheriff was working at night near several bars. He observed two cars emerge from a parking lot in a reckless manner at excessive speeds. They passed his marked vehicle and entered the highway side by side. The highway was mountainous, narrow, sharply curved and heavily traveled. Although the deputy was in pursuit and had the authority to apprehend the motorists for the offenses which they were committing, he did not signal them to stop. One of the cars collided head-on with another vehicle, killing five occupants and completely disabling the sixth. In a suit for damages, the deputy was dismissed as a defendant. The court reasoned that the deputy owed no duty to the deceased and the injured. His obligation to enforce the law was to society in general; only a criminal prosecution of the deputy could redress any breach of his duty (160).

Civil disorders present difficult questions to agencies concerning proper tactics. Failure to act is one charge flung at departments. A group of Miami, Florida proprietors sued the city for injury to

160. *Massengill v. Yuma Co.,* 104 Ariz. 518, 456 P. 2d 376, 41 A.L.R. 3d 692 (1969).

their businesses during riots at the 1968 Republican Convention. After they demanded and received extra police patrols, the mayor and sheriff decided that tensions would be eased if officers were taken away. Following this maneuver, burning and looting erupted. The court denied responsibility of the city for the damages. No special obligation to protect petitioners was established, even though the authorities originally had responded to pleas for additional manpower. The opinion pointed out that police had the right to exercise discretion as to strategy. Plaintiffs did not prove that more harm had resulted from removing the officers than would have occurred had they remained (161).

Law enforcement agencies are not insurers of the safety of individuals. Their responsibility runs to the people. Even in high crime areas, departments are not required to anticipate that any particular citizen will be harmed.

A novel theory by taxpayers in a California suit may suggest a remedy to those who complain of lack of protection. Petitioners sued a sheriff under a statute allowing resident taxpayers to enjoin illegal expenditures of public funds. They questioned his enforcement of an allegedly unconstitutional law. This rationale could be molded into a challenge of troop deployment in riots or resource management throughout a district (162).

In an Indiana case a merchant sued the municipality, claiming that he was driven out of business by the refusal of the city to combat crime in his neighborhood. Relying on governmental immunity and the rule that the duty to protect is to the public, the court held that the city was insulated from liability (163).

Sometimes an apparent failure to act amounts to negligent performance. One example is the refusal of a jailer to remove a convict from a cell shared with a felon who has a history of assaulting cellmates. Many successful suits have been brought by inmates who suffered aggravated injuries due to lack of medical treatment. In these cases a special relationship exists between guard and prisoner because of the control of one over the other.

161. *Wong v. Miami,* 7 Cr. L. 2294 (Fla. Sup. Ct. 1970).
162. *Blair v. Pitchess,* 96 Cal. Rptr. 42, 486 P. 2d 1242 (1971).
163. *Simpson's Food Fair, Inc. v. City of Evansville,* 272 N.E. 2d 871 (Ind. App. 1971).

EXCEPTIONS

As with any general rule, this one has its exceptions. For example, if a patrolman saw a man beating another and made no effort to halt the battery when he could have done so, liability would surely follow. Also, when an officer begins to perform and unreasonably ceases, a duty is inferred toward one whose injuries would have been decreased if the officer had responded. In other situations a special relationship emerges between law enforcer and plaintiff creating an obligation to act.

Officers are not absolved of a duty to protect a man whom they requested to identify four arrested suspects. An Illinois decision said that the patrolmen were obligated to plaintiff to prevent the arrestees from harming him. Plaintiff was a chaperone at a teenage dance. Four drunks burst into the hall and were ordered out. When plaintiff called the police, the drunks attacked him and threatened his life. An hour later they were seized by several officers. Plaintiff was asked to identify those who had been apprehended. In the process, the policemen let go of the assailants who fell upon plaintiff and hurt him (164).

A duty to one man may emerge if there is a special relationship between him and the department. Such a tie was found by a New York court. Willie Sutton, a dangerous fugitive, was the subject of a manhunt. A young man saw Sutton and informed the authorities. The youth's part in Sutton's apprehension was widely publicized. Threats on the informant's life were reported to the police. Adequate safeguards were refused. Three weeks later he was shot to death. His estate won a judgment against the municipality based on its failure to protect him. He had collaborated with the police in the arrest of Sutton and reasonably demanded protection when he was imperiled. Thus, a duty arose for the city to guard his safety (165).

Subsequently, the New York courts distinguished another citizen's right to protection from the special relationship in the Sutton apprehension and withheld liability. A girl had been terrorized for more than six months; a spurned suitor threatened

---

164. *Gardner v. Village of Chicago Ridge,* 128 Ill. App. 2d 157, 262 N.E. 2d 829 (1970).
165. *Schuster v. City of N. Y.,* 180 N.Y.S. 2d 265, 154 N.E. 2d 534 (1958).

to kill or maim her. Repeated pleas to the police for help were denied. Following her engagement to someone else and a last chance warning from the rejected suitor, she implored the authorities to assist her. Again they refused to protect her. The next day a thug, hired by her former lover, threw lye in her face. She was permanently scarred and blinded in one eye. After this attack, round-the-clock policemen were assigned to her for three and one-half years. On these facts, the court said that she had no enforceable right to special protection and ruled in favor of the city (166).

A lower New York court was more sympathetic in the early stages of another such claim. Plaintiff contended that he needed information from the municipality so that he could frame a complaint on breach of the public trust to defend persons injured in a riot. He obtained an order to examine city records on police performance during the disturbance (167).

A federal opinion ruled that protection is owed to an endangered informant. Plaintiff told Internal Revenue Service agents about certain whiskey offenses. The alleged criminal, a man with a reputation for violence, learned of plaintiff's role as informant and threatened him. The warning was communicated to the I.R.S. Plaintiff relied upon their assurance that he was safe. However, three days before a scheduled appearance before a grand jury, plaintiff's home was bombed and he was hurt. Even though the trial court said that the government negligently breached its duty to protect, relief to plaintiff was denied because there was no proof that the breach was the proximate cause of his injury. The court discussed the Sutton case and distinguished that informant, who was a young man without a record, from this informant, who had a felony record and an unsavory background. Many persons had motives to attack this fellow; no enemies of Sutton's informant were disclosed. However, upon appeal the case was reversed with a holding for plaintiff on the basis that the government did not show that plaintiff's other enemies bombed the house (168).

166. *Riss v. City of N.Y.*, 22 N.Y. 2d 579, 240 N.E. 2d 860 (1968).

167. *Matter of De Vito*, 4 Cr. L. 2146 (N.Y.C. Ct. 1968).

168. *Swanner v. U.S.*, 275 F. Supp. 1007 (M.D. Ala. 1967); rev'd, 406 F. 2d 716 (5th Cir. 1969).

LEGISLATION TO BENEFIT VICTIMS OF CRIME

Legislation exists in many areas to recompense innocent victims of violent crimes. Such laws are one answer to the doctrine that these persons have no enforceable claim against policemen or governments. Payment to such victims was authorized in some of the earliest legal codes and is being enacted today. A bill has been introduced in Congress to compensate those harmed by criminal violence in federal jurisdictions, such as the District of Columbia.

One version of such statutes allows recovery to people hurt by mob violence or riots. Without specific guidelines for the incidents covered by these laws, courts vary in construing the provisions. For example, how many persons constitute a mob? The answers range from at least three to twelve or more. An element of some legislation is that the mob be taking the law into its own hands, such as in a lynching.

A Kansas case filed under a mob action statute illustrates the wide scope of these provisions. A wife parked her car in the hospital parking lot while visiting her husband in the hospital. Upon returning she was pulled out of the vehicle into a waiting car where five men raped and abused her for two hours. They drove her to another area and forceably entered a dwelling. She was ravished by several different men. Afterwards, she was dragged across a field and into a building and again raped. She sued the city under the mob action law and won. The court said that this incident was one for which the statute had been designed; the number of people and the public disturbance amounted to mob action (169).

So long as compensation is available to innocent victims of crime, probably no outcry will be heard to alter the general rule that they have no remedy against officers. For several years the focus of change in criminal law has been toward humane treatment and constitutional liberties for the accused. Certainly this trend was necessary, but attention is now centering on the innocent victim and his legitimate needs.

---

169. *Jackson v. Kansas City, Kansas,* 448 F. 2d 518 (10th Cir. 1971).

PRIVATE POLICE

The relationship of private police forces and their employers is different from that between public officers and individual citizens. In the former the obligation of protection is established by contract. Violation of the terms is breach of contract; ordinary rules of contract apply. Usually an agreement provides for reasonable measures to safeguard the employer or others. Without a specific clause insuring that no harm will befall the employer, the private security force does not guarantee safety. Some factors which affect court decisions are reasonableness of preventive measures, forseeability of harm, proximate cause and intervening cause. Obviously the employment arrangement must be examined in each situation. The agreement need not be in writing. Oral contracts are as binding as written ones, although the terms may be more difficult to prove.

CONCLUSION

A duty is not owed by officers and governments to protect any particular individual. The obligation to enforce the law and apprehend violators benefits the public, not a specific person. This is the general rule. Exceptions arise when a special relationship develops between authorities and plaintiff. Examples occur when the hazard is due to cooperation with the police, when officers stand by and refuse aid which could have prevented the harm or when there is exclusive control over the injured person.

CHAPTER FIFTEEN

SUITS BY PRISONERS

IMPRISONMENT does not divest an inmate of all of his rights, although they are diminished in comparison with those of a free citizen. Courts, in the past, have followed a hands-off policy except in extremely aggravated situations. But enough instances of tyranny have been presented that judges now accept jurisdiction of many prisoner complaints.

There have been many hurdles to such litigation. Courts are loathe to interfere in prison management and are cognizant of the need for discipline. State statutes provide for civil death of inmates thereby prohibiting them from filing suits. However, constitutional pleas cannot be so barred and, as seen in Chapter Eleven, most pertinent grievances can be drafted in constitutional language.

Courts have not hesitated to declare prison facilities unfit for humans. These decisions are just beginning and will increase dramatically as the results become public. In essence, judges rule that punitive measures which shock the conscience will not be permitted. Punishment that is utterly disproportionate to the crime for which the inmate is confined is cruel and unusual.

As penal theory moves toward rehabilitation and away from punishment, judgments will include relief from unduly harsh handling and directives for helpful procedures. Courts are looking at limitations on visitations, correspondence, educational aids, access to judicial relief and exercise of religion.

Jailers have a duty to exercise ordinary care for the safety of prisoners. If injury from jailers' conduct or failure to act is foreseeable, they will be held responsible. Harm inflicted by fellow inmates falls into this category. If the damage could have been anticipated, there will be liability.

FAILURE OF CARE

Two prisoners sued under the federal tort claims act to recover damages from the United States for personal injuries sustained at a federal prison by reason of the negligence of a government employee. The statute waives sovereign immunity for negligence of federal employees. Prior cases had held that no such relief was available; however, the United States Supreme Court decided that suits by federal inmates are within the purview of the act. The allegations in the first case were that the prison employees were negligent in failing to provide medical care resulting in delayed removal of a brain tumor and blindness. The inmate had suffered from dizziness, loss of balance and difficulty with vision. His symptoms were erroneously evaluated and virtually untreated. Almost a year later, a consulting physician examined him and correctly diagnosed a tumor. A subsequent operation removed a brain tumor which had caused the problems.

The second case related to an attack on a prisoner by twelve inmates who pursued him into a dormitory. A guard, apparently choosing to confine the altercation instead of interceding, locked the dormitory. Plaintiff was beaten by the assailants until unconscious. His skull was fractured, and he lost the sight of one eye. He contended that prison officials were negligent in failing to provide enough guards to supervise the inmates and to prevent assaults. The court ruled that, since the federal tort claims act encompasses suits by federal prisoners, the United States will be liable if its employees acted negligently (170).

Plaintiff's husband was incarcerated in a Florida town in a helpless condition because of intoxication. The jailer locked all the doors and departed, leaving no attendant on duty. During the night the jail filled with smoke resulting in the asphyxiation of plaintiff's husband. Plaintiff sued the city for damages for the negligence of the jailer. The court ruled that the municipality could be liable for the jailer's wrongful conduct (171).

The widow of a former inmate sued the surety on the bond of a

170. *U.S. v. Muniz,* 374 U.S. 150, 10 L. Ed. 2d 805, 83 S. Ct. 1850 (1963).

171. *Hargrove v. Town of Cocoa Beach,* 96 So. 2d 130, 60 A.L.R. 2d 1193 (Fla. 1957).

Georgia prison warden. Her husband died as a result of a dynamite explosion at a rock quarry. He and a fellow prisoner were directed to load dynamite into a hole which had been drilled in a rock ledge. After placing about nine sticks inside, the dynamite hung up. The guard ordered decedent to pour additional dynamite inside. When this maneuver failed to dislodge the sticks, the guard directed the inmates to force the drill into the hole against the dynamite. An explosion killed plaintiff's husband. She alleged that the guard knew that the drill would trigger an explosion and that his actions were in direct violation of rules and regulations of the Georgia penal system. The warden, and the guard as his subordinate, were covered by the bond. Proof of these contentions will result in recovery for plaintiff (172).

Plaintiff asserts that he lost control of his automobile and ran off the highway. His neck was broken in the accident. An Alabama sheriff arrested plaintiff and locked him up. Despite repeated requests for medical attention or the use of the telephone to call a physician, he was incarcerated for 23 hours. Upon release, he immediately obtained medical help. His injuries were diagnosed as two dislocated and one fractured cranial vertebrae. He was hospitalized and in traction for 15 days and wore a brace for five months. If plaintiff proves these allegations, he will establish a compensable claim under the civil rights act (173).

RIGHT TO COUNSEL

Plaintiff, sentenced to 20 to 30 years in a New York state prison, sued two county police officers under the civil rights act. His complaint alleged that they denied him assistance of counsel after arrest, brutally pummelled him at the police station, threatened to kill him, obtained a purported identification of him from the victim in violation of due process standards, secured incriminating oral statements from him by beating him and testified falsely at the criminal trial. Defendants filed a motion to dismiss asserting that New York law suspends all of plaintiff's civil rights during his incarceration in a state prison; therefore, he

172. *Fidelity-Phenix Ins. Co. v. Mauldin,* 118 Ga. App. 401, 163 S.E. 2d 834 (1968).
173. *Hughes v. Noble,* 295 F.2d 495 (5th Cir. 1961).

cannot pursue this federal remedy. Motion to dismiss was denied. The court stressed that a suit under the civil rights act could be brought by a prisoner despite the state civil death section. Whether plaintiff's contentions are supportable will depend upon evidence at a trial (174).

ASSAULT AND BATTERY

Plaintiff sued an Oregon sheriff and his deputy. Plaintiff contended that he was forced into a cell with unnecessary brutality which resulted in a broken jaw. Defendants' version was that no force was used until plaintiff had twice kicked at the deputy who was trying to put him into a cell. The deputy admitted that he hit plaintiff once with his fist. The injury apparently arose from contact between plaintiff's head and the interior of the cell. Because of contradictory testimony there were questions for jury resolution as to self-defense. The verdict was for defendants; it was affirmed on appeal (175).

CRUELTY

Plaintiffs were arrested in Mississippi for marching without a parade permit. The protestors were detained at the city auditorium for several hours. Some of them were children and were released to their parents; others were freed on bonds of $200 or on their own recognizance. Those remaining, filling three commercial buses, were removed to a state penitentiary 215 miles away. No arrangements were made to take them before a magistrate so that he might determine whether they should be held. Mississippi statutes require that every person making an arrest shall take the offender before the proper officer without unnecessary delay. Although the police chief was aware of this provision and knew that posting bond had nothing to do with this law, he had contrived a rule that no one would be taken before a magistrate who had not posted bond. After unsuccessful attempts to locate jail space for plaintiffs in Natchez and nearby

174. *Beyer v. Werner,* 299 F. Supp. 967 (D.C. N.Y. 1969).
175. *Roskop v. Trent,* 443 P.2d 174 (Or. 1968).

communities, the chief arranged for their incarceration in the state prison. The last of the plaintiffs made bond and left the penitentiary five days after arrival.

The prison superintendent placed plaintiffs in a section of the facility reserved for incorrigible felons. All procedures which applied to such inmates were utilized against plaintiffs although they had only been arrested and not yet convicted of a crime for which the maximum punishment was a fine of $300 or 90 days' imprisonment. Each person was compelled to take a laxative upon admission to maximum security. Male prisoners were deprived of their clothing. Females were allowed to wear underwear and dresses but no shoes, stockings or coats. Six to eight persons were placed in two bunk cells with no place to sleep except the bare metal beds or the floor. Minimal hygenic needs were not supplied. The court directed verdicts against the police chief for failing to take plaintiffs before a magistrate and against the superintendent for denial of due process of law (176).

Plaintiff, an inmate of Clinton State Prison in New York, sued under the civil rights act for an injunction and damages for cruel and unusual punishment in violation of the Eighth Amendment. The court ruled that if his allegations were proven, his rights had been violated by prison officials. He had been placed in solitary confinement for 11 days without any clothing; the cell was empty except for a toilet and sink which was encrusted with slime, dirt and human excrement; he was not furnished soap, towel, toilet paper, toothbrush or other hygenic implements; he was forced to stand at attention whenever guards appeared from 7:30 a.m. to 10:00 p.m. under threat of physical violence for disobedience; the windows were opened wide throughout the evening and night even though the temperature was subfreezing. After 11 days of these conditions he was given underwear. Other conditions were unchanged for an additional 22 days. A year later he was again placed in a strip cell for 21 days for violating a prison rule. He received no advance notice of the charges against him and had no opportunity to defend himself.

Prison officials posed three technical defenses to the claims.

176. *Anderson v. Nosser,* 456 F. 2d 835 (5th Cir. 1972).

First they contended that the Eighth Amendment does not apply to the states but only to the federal government. The court ruled that there is no longer any question that the Eighth Amendment does apply to states. Second, that courts should not interfere in internal discipline of state prisons. On this point, the decision stated that judges are sensitive to the needs of prisons for discipline, but they will not hesitate to intervene in appropriate cases such as the present one. Third, that state remedies must be sought before turning to federal relief. Federal courts have concurrent jurisdiction for cases involving constitutional rights, and in this situation state remedies are inadequate (177).

A fourteen year old plaintiff was convicted of petty larceny for taking articles with a retail value of $2.11. He was sentenced to 90 days at a county farm in Mississippi. The farm was administered by defendant, an experienced officer. The inmates served their sentences by working on public projects. A trusty system was employed by which certain inmates had special privileges and responsibilities; some acted as armed guards. On the day in question the *shooter* was a 23 year old with a fourth grade education, serving time for assault and battery with intent to kill. He was furnished a 12 gauge shotgun and a quantity of shells containing 7 1/2 shot. He was in charge when the prisoners stopped for lunch. Plaintiff was resting on the ground about 50 feet from where the guard stood with the weapon cradled under the arm. Without any warning, the gun fired directly into plaintiff's face, causing blindness in both eyes, brain damage and other injuries resulting in total and permanent disability. The guard was unable to satisfactorily explain why the gun fired; apparently it was not defective. He had received virtually no training or safety instructions before being made an armed trusty.

Plaintiff sued the municipal judge, the sheriff, the surety, the county board of supervisors and the superintendent of the farm. Only the latter was held liable. The superintendent had a legal duty to exercise reasonable care for the safety of the prisoners. The evidence clearly demonstrated failure of the superintendent to use proper care in turning over to this trusty a loaded gun without

177. *Wright v. McMann*, 387 F. 2d 519 (2nd Cir. 1967).

making certain that he was competent to handle it. The superintendent violated his responsibility under state law and he exerted cruel and unusual punishment upon plaintiff in deprivation of his Eighth Amendment rights. Imprisonment under the extra hazardous conditions to which plaintiff was needlessly exposed and which culminated in permanently maiming and totally disabling him was so utterly disproportionate to his crime as to constitute cruel and inhuman punishment (178).

INJURIES INFLICTED BY FELLOW PRISONERS

Plaintiff was arrested by Lexington, Kentucky police and taken to the holdover at the station. Almost immediately thereafter a 260 pound prisoner attacked and injured plaintiff. No official was present during the assault. Shortly thereafter, another inmate and the turnkey came to his rescue. The attacker had been arrested for drunkenness in a public place. There was no evidence that he had a propensity for violence. The court ruled that no fault of the jailer was established. The duty of a jailer toward a person in custody is to exercise ordinary care to prevent unlawful injury. He cannot be liable for negligence in failing to prevent what he could not reasonably anticipate. A jailer is not an insurer of the safety of prisoners under his control (179).

Plaintiff was confined for drunkenness in a Kentucky county jail. He was placed in a bullpen into which a number of cells opened. Several prisoners were locked in the bullpen without being assigned or confined to a cell. The cell doors were not locked. Plaintiff was assaulted by another prisoner, a convicted murderer, who had been in the jail for almost a year before the incident. The jailer was aware that the man had beaten up other inmates. The court held that a jury should decide whether the jailer was negligent in not segregating the assailant from other prisoners. There was evidence to support liability for the jailer's acts (180).

Two individuals, confined in a Missouri county jail, sued the

---

178. *Roberts v. Williams,* 302 F. Supp. 972 (N.D. Miss. 1969).
179. *City of Lexington v. Greenhow,* 451 S.W. 2d 424, 41 A.L.R. 3d 1018 (Ky. 1970).
180. *Glover v. Hazelwood,* 387 S.W. 2d 600 (Ky. 1965).

sheriff, chief deputy and their surety for actual and punitive damages for injuries received from fellow prisoners. They asserted that defendants knowingly permitted hardened criminals to conduct a kind of kangeroo court which abused and harmed plaintiffs. Afterwards they were refused requested medical aid. Other contentions were that defendants neglected to make reasonable inspection of cells to check the well-being of prisoners and failed to properly select and train employees. The court ruled that, if the allegations were proven, they would constitute breach of defendants' duties to faithfully perform their office and thereby establish liability on the official bond (181).

FREEDOM OF RELIGION

Four inmates in California's Folsome State Prison sued the warden and "John Does" for systematic harrassment against the exercise of the Black Muslim religion. Defendants were alleged to have obstructed plaintiffs' right to worship God by insulting them, confining them to a segregated unit of the prison with the loss of credits and good time, and additional penalties. No other inmates were placed in solitary confinement for praying, or punished for the practice of their religious beliefs. The trial court dismissed the petition, but on appeal the judgment was reversed. Plaintiffs were entitled to a hearing. At trial the court must consider the effect that practice of the Black Muslim religion will have upon the maintenence of prison order and discipline as well as the administrative difficulties involved in permitting the exercise of this religion within prison walls (182).

PRISON CONDITIONS

Patients at the Treatment Center of the Massachusetts Correctional Institution sued state officials under the civil rights act, claiming that the Eighth Amendment was violated because of grossly inadequate heating leading to physical ills and severe personal discomfort. The sole relief sought was an order to supply

181. *Miller v. Owsley,* 422 S.W. 2d 39 (Mo. 1967).
182. *Williford v. Peo. of Calif.,* 352 F. 2d 474 (9th Cir. 1965).

adequate heat. Defendants contended that the deficiency in the heating was unintentional. They were doing the best that they could under the circumstances. The facility was old, and there were no controls to regulate excessive heat in some portions and insufficient steam in other areas. Also, the defense was asserted that because plaintiffs were confined prior to trial, as distinguished from after conviction, they were not entitled to claim cruel and unusual punishment. The court disagreed with the latter argument and opined that personal good faith of the individual defendants is not a defense to this complaint. Plaintiffs did not have to show that the authorities purposely deprived them of heat. The result, not specific intent, is what matters. Human needs and constitutional requirements are not to be measured or limited by dollar considerations (183).

Inmates of a Philadelphia prison sued officials under the civil rights act. Two years earlier the same court had found despicable conditions in the facility; incarceration there of untried arrestees who were unable to make bond constituted cruel and unusual punishment. In the instant case a three-judge panel ruled that the entire Philadelphia penal system violated the First, Sixth, Eighth and Fourteenth Amendments to the United States Constitution, a clause of the Pennsylvania constitution, the civil rights act, four state statutes and the Philadelphia home rule charter. The court pointed to the poor status and inferior design of the buildings, crowding of prisoners, sparsity of guards, filth, rat-infested kitchens, inadequate food, lack of medical care and absence of rehabilitative or recreational programs. The court described these prisons as degrading and disgusting places which are likely to bring out the worst in the men incarcerated therein. The court ordered defendants to undertake immediate correction of those conditions which could be remedied relatively quickly and economically and to formulate plans to alter those matters which are of a long range nature. Defendants were directed to report their accomplishments to the court within short intervals. Jurisdiction of the case was retained to supervise further developments (184).

183. *Rozecki v. Gaughan,* 459 F. 2d 6 (1st Cir. 1972).

184. *Jackson v. Hendrick,* 11 Cr. L. 2088 (Pa. Ct. Comm. Pls. 1972).

CONCLUSION

A new field of litigation has opened in suits by prisoners. Supervisors who silently acquiesce in maltreatment of inmates, as well as those directly involved in such conduct, are faulted. An obligation to act is created by the helplessness of the one incarcerated; his ability to take care of himself is diminished. Recent decisions have expanded the range of complaints. No longer do grievances mainly focus on assault and battery situations; today, prisoner suits run the gamut of complaints against law enforcers.

CHAPTER SIXTEEN

PRIVATE POLICE

MOST types of complaints that are filed against law enforcers could also be initiated against private police. Several other chapters contain cases involving private investigators. Many principles applicable to liability of officers are pertinent. But, unless authorized by law, private investigators have only the powers of citizens. This chapter delves into particular situations in which nonpublic forces have been challenged.

Statutes are vitally important in determining the status of private investigators. Their privileges to carry weapons, etc., may be set out in enactments or administrative regulations. Also, many jurisdictions have legislated specific provisions for such crimes as shoplifting. The right to detain suspects often is greater in these violations than in other offenses.

Suits under the federal civil rights act cannot be brought against private individuals. However, if a detective is also a policeman or has been empowered to fulfill general law enforcement functions, he may be acting as an officer rather than as a citizen.

Some decisions are included on loss of license. This civil penalty against defendant may be of greater significance than would be a monetary award to a plaintiff.

LOSS OF LICENSE

A private investigator was convicted of the misdemeanor of conspiracy to alter the racing performance of a horse or to mislead persons as the the true identity of a horse entered in a contest. This amounts to fraud since unsuspecting individuals wagering on or against the animal would be relying upon its normal ability or its supposed identity. Based upon this conviction the detective's license was revoked. Grounds for cancelling such license include conviction of a felony or a crime involving moral turpitude. The offense itself is a felony; conspiracy to commit the crime is a misdemeanor. In an appeal of the administrative decision, the court affirmed because the investigator had been convicted of a crime involving moral turpitude (185).

Three employees of a licensed New York detective agency raided an apartment early one morning to obtain evidence for a divorce proceeding. Their client's husband was in the apartment with another woman. The detectives employed the ruse of delivering a telegram to induce the apartment dweller to open the door. As the woman retrieved the alleged message, six people forced their way inside by breaking the chain lock. They had not requested permission to enter. For about 40 minutes they pushed and shoved the dweller, took photographs and broke her possessions. The woman claimed that the agency invaded her privacy and unlawfully searched her premises. The latter claim was based upon the New York civil rights law which applies both to policemen and private individuals. The New York authorities suspended the agency's license for a period of two months (186).

The Bureau of Private Investigators and Adjustors in California charged an agency with dishonesty and fraud and suspended its license for 90 days. This decision was affirmed on appeal. Six different incidents were outlined in the complaint. In each one, an agent had contacted an automobile accident witness whose interests were adverse to that of the client. When the witness asked for identification, the investigator did not disclose that he represented the opposing side but instead answered evasively, implying that he was associated with the witness's insurer. Although there was no active misrepresentation that the investigator was from an interviewee's company, deception was standard practice to overcome the difficulty of securing a statement from such witnesses. This conduct was intended deliberately to trick the unwary into thinking that the investigator was acting on behalf of their insurer. This constitutes fraud and dishonesty under the

---

185. *Otash v. Bur. of Pri. Investigators and Adjusters,* 41 Cal. Rptr. 263 (1964).

186. *Agency for Investigation and Detection, Inc. v. Dept. of State,* 25 A.D. 2d 738, 269 N.Y.S. 2d 168 (1966).

statute authorizing suspension of a private investigator's license (187).

PRIVACY

Plaintiff sued an insurance company for invasion of right of privacy. She alleged that defendant caused her to be openly shadowed by a private investigator after she had instituted a personal injury suit against defendant. The detective hired by defendant took moves to discover if there were any inconsistency between the injuries which plaintiff claimed and her actual physical activity. The defendant answered that the surveillance was done in secret. Because of the dispute concerning the facts, the court ruled that the case should be heard on the merits. Plaintiff must expect a reasonable investigation of her claim, but defendant is not permitted to harrass or intimidate a person being investigated. The fact that the detective was inadvertently observed by plaintiff is not in itself enough to cause liability (188).

FIREARMS

Plaintiff, an innocent bystander, was hit by a bullet fired by a private guard. The latter shot into the air over the head of a suspect running at 2:00 a.m. from a closed cafe protected by the shooter's employer. The wounded man sued the private patrolman. A judgment awarding damages was entered by stipulation. Then plaintiff sued the agency's surety. The bond, conditioned on the faithful and honest performance by the agency of the business of private detective, authorized those injured by the willful, malicious or wrongful act of the agency to sue on the bond. The court held that unfaithful conduct meant everything that the law does not permit or excuse. Negligence is not faithful performance and includes a wrongful act and an omission to use due care. Therefore, the reckless shot by the guard was covered under the

187. *Wayne v. Bur. of Pri. Investigators and Adjusters,* 20 Cal. Rptr. 194 (1962).

188. *Tucker v. Am. Employers' Ins. Co.,* 171 So. 2d 437, 13 A.L.R. 3d 1020 (Fla. App. 1965).

bond (189).

FALSE ARREST AND IMPRISONMENT

A patron sought damages for false arrest, false imprisonment, assault and battery from a Rhode Island racetrack and a racing protective association. Plaintiff was a 70 per cent disabled veteran with a mental age of a ten year old. He slipped a companion a five dollar bill at a food vending stand, whereupon two detectives ordered both men to accompany them to the office of the association. The investigators were part-time employees who also held high ranks as city policemen. Plaintiff contended that he was involuntarily detained, questioned and then forceably expelled from the track. He was escorted on a flight of stairs, pushed down and forced out a gate that was some distance from his car, despite having vomited and obviously being unnerved. After these incidents, his disability increased from 70 to 100 per cent. The detectives testified that plaintiff was not confined in any manner, was not touched and could have left them if he pleased. However, they evicted plaintiff because of his boisterousness. The jury apparently believed plaintiff's version of the occurrence and rendered a verdict for him against both the track and the association. Although by statute there was authority to eject an undesirable customer, there was no legal justification for detention. Liability for false imprisonment was upheld on appeal (190).

A customer of a discount house in Missouri sued the business for false imprisonment. Plaintiff, aged 79, and his fiancee went in to purchase wedding rings. A security station was set up near the entrance. A sign on the desk stated that packages were to be tagged and examined by a guard. The latter was instructed to mark incoming bundles with tags and check outgoing packages for either such tags or cash register slips but never to touch the customers. Plaintiff and his fiancee bought two rings which were placed in a sack with a receipt attached. As they approached the front door, a guard grabbed plaintiff's arm, removed the package and took it to the desk to look at it. To plaintiff's explanation that he had paid

189. *Callum v. Hartford Acc. and Indemnity Co.*, 337 P.2d 259 (Cal. App. 1959).

190. *Webbier v. Thoroughbred Racing Protective Bur., Inc.*, 254 A. 2d 285 (R. I. 1969).

for the goods, the guard replied that the container was not properly tagged. Plaintiff returned to the jewelry counter where he was informed that the sack was correctly marked. The clerk told the guard to let plaintiff leave. The episode consumed about 15 minutes; the detention lasted 5 or 6 minutes. Two of plaintiff's acquaintances saw the events and possibly twenty-five or thirty persons were in the vicinity. He recovered for mental suffering, injury to his reputation and punitive damages for malice implied from the guard's reckless failure to respect plaintiff's rights (191).

Plaintiff entered a department store in Kansas City, Missouri to buy swim trunks and film. No clerk was near the men's clothing racks and he was in a hurry, so he removed a pair of trunks and carried them over his arm to the camera counter. While there, a Kansas City officer, who was working as a store detective during his off-duty hours, accosted plaintiff for having the goods without intending to pay for them. After he tried to explain the circumstances, he was directed to walk down to the manager's office. The detective told the manager that plaintiff was a shoplifter. He was interrogated and asked to sign a confession. When he refused, the detective called the police. Plaintiff was arrested and carried to the station. He was confined in the manager's office for about an hour and at the station for approximately three hours before being freed on bond. For two hours he had been locked up with other prisoners. The detective testified that plaintiff hid the trunks and evasively answered inquiries about his conduct. On conflicting evidence, the jury gave plaintiff actual and punitive damages. The detective was acting on behalf of the store; therefore, it was liable for false arrest. Humiliation and embarassment substantiated the judgment for actual damages. Punitive damages were awarded both as punishment and deterrent to defendant (192).

Plaintiff sued an insurer and its special agent for false imprisonment. Plaintiff was working in a cafe when a deputy state fire marshal and an insurance investigator showed her a badge and demanded that she accompany them to answer some questions. They carried her to the police chief's office and accused her of

191. *Garvis v. K Mart Discount Store,* 461 S. W. 2d 317 (Mo. App. 1970).
192. *Nelson v. R. H. Macy and Co.,* 434 S. W. 2d 767 (Mo. App. 1969).

setting fire to a house she owned. They took her there against her will and detained her for about 2 1/2 hours. During the interrogation she was accused of lying and repeatedly told that they would send her to the penitentiary. They would not let her leave although many times she said that she had to return to the cafe. When released she was too nervous to work and became sick for several days. The insurance agent initiated the investigation; the deputy fire marshal was assisting him. The Texas court decided that plaintiff had established false imprisonment for which the investigator and his employer could be responsible (193).

CONCLUSION

Private police are exposed to liability on many of the same types of cases which have led to judgments against officers. Reported decisions involving private police mostly deal with improper surveillance and mistreatment of suspected shoplifters. However, other complaints illustrate the kinds of risks which these agents face. Even if private police are not sued, misconduct may lead to loss of license.

193. *American Ins. Ass'n v. Smith,* 439 S. W. 2d 418 (Tex. App. 1969).

PART THREE
ALTERNATIVES TO CIVIL LIABILITY

CHAPTER SEVENTEEN

OVERVIEW OF ALTERNATIVES

CIVIL liability of officers poses a dilemma to policemen, to complainants and to the community. The latter requires officers who are undaunted and who will respond promptly to incidents. Fear of judgments for misconduct could induce excessive caution and impede aggressive enforcement. Those wronged by police action should have a just remedy. However, the future of an officer, and that of his family, should not be in jeopardy when he performs public services.

The problem boils down to a balancing of interests. How can these apparently opposing needs be satisfied? Surely the lawsuits in Part Two demonstrate that courts do not rush into judgments against law enforcers. Courts translate conflicting allegations into awards or dismissals. But solutions often are belated and inappropriate. Also, the cases illustrate that courts in one state may decide a claim differently from the way another tribunal has ruled in the past. Some of the disparity in relief to citizens of various states has been equalized by federal jurisdiction under the civil rights act. In any event, courts redress individual complaints and are not a forum for more comprehensive remedies which might prevent future conflicts.

Traditionally, the defense available to law enforcement has been sovereign immunity. Although this ancient doctrine is fast being abolished by courts and legislatures, (194) in many areas it still clothes agencies and some officers. However, for a particular policeman governmental immunity usually evaporates if he acted outside the scope of his authority. Since most conduct for which an officer is liable is beyond this limit, the defense has been of little worth to the man in the field. Nonetheless, governmental immunity is no answer; at best it is only the immovable object to

194. R.C.W.A. (Wash) § §4.92.090 and 4.96.010 (see Appendix).

the irresistable force of wronged claimants.

Another approach to shielding an officer from liability has been indemnification. By statute in some states, (195) after a policeman has been found responsible for damages related to the performance of his duties, his employer pays the recovery. Other measures for accomplishing similar results are comprehensive insurance coverage or surety bonds. Purchase of such policies acknowledges that an officer is a public servant and that damages arising from his activities should be borne by society. This principle is prevalent in modern tort law under even less obvious circumstances. Enterprise liability is a current term for the cost to a manufacturer of injuries to those who use its wares. Such amounts become part of the cost of doing business. For example, General Motors Corporation pays damages to persons harmed by its defective vehicles.

An aspect of police civil litigation that has not been stressed is the expense to everyone involved, including the public. This cost is not measured alone in dollars. Some other facets of the burden are anxiety of policemen, estrangement of citizens, overburdening the judiciary, and the time of all parties and witnesses. Assets should be better utilized. Insights, of course, have sprung from the focus that civil lawsuits have brought upon police practices. But now that this spotlight has illumined the disease, cures should be sought.

The ideal solution concerning claims of those hurt by policemen is to prevent the injuries. The old adage that an ounce of prevention is worth a pound of cure fits officer-citizen confrontations. Facts are detailed throughout Part Two to explicitly demonstrate which incidents have led to plaintiffs' verdicts and which to defendants' exonerations. Following the lessons of these cases will decrease clashes.

Pride has been the genesis of many confrontations. In the past a policeman's pride has been symbolized by the trappings of his office. Anyone foolish enough to defy him or show disrespect for his status courted arrest and abuse. "Move along, boy," in a southern town or "alley court" in an urban environment have substituted for lawful procedures. Questioning officialdom is

195. Rev. Stat. Neb. 1943 §23-1716 (see Appendix).

typical of modern society. A policeman must have the courage to back down if he has assumed an indefensible position. Hopefully, an education will help him to shun such postures. A billy club is no answer to legitimate inquiry. One of the slogans embodied on colonial flags in the American Revolution was "Don't Tread on Me." Civil litigation against officers has been an overt method of enforcing this motto.

Many thoughtful critics have examined the police function. Much of their commentary relates to preventing the entanglements that lead to suits against policemen. Alienation of law enforcers from the community at large is widely discussed. Lack of tolerance prevails on all sides. Realistically, who can deny that society needs law enforcement and that officers cannot function effectively without citizen assistance? Neither an armed nor a terrified citizenry is feasible in a democratic system.

This segment of the book will suggest alternatives to civil litigation: both methods to prevent conflicts and to handle complaints. Public relations and community involvement are programs that can be immediately implemented by departments of all sizes. Tension filled encounters should not be the only meetings for citizens and their police. The good samaritan in blue and the officer as protector of life and property must be revealed. The community should be included in making some strategic choices. Effort should be directed toward discovering how the community wants to be policed. If police problems are openly presented to citizens, a wave of cooperation may transform mountains into molehills.

Administrative processing of complaints is an alternative to judicial settlement. Public funds could be allocated for speedy payment of proper claims. Evaluation of improper police practices could be made by a civilian review board, an ombudsman or a police unit. Development of better procedures could come from such scrutiny. Recommendations for discipline of misbehaving officers could be made to department chiefs who would be in charge of punishment and implementation of new techniques.

The ultimate answer to diminishing citizen-officer clashes is better selection of applicants and education of policemen. The selection process should weed out unfit persons. Some individuals cannot handle the authority that a policeman wields. Others are incompetent for different reasons: mental, physical and emotional. A citizen cannot be transformed into a professional peace officer by donning a uniform and undergoing a quickie course in police methods. He must be educated to an awareness of the proper exercise of his awesome power and to a respect for the rights of each individual.

CONCLUSION

Civil liability lawsuits are one technique for rectifying wrongs. Now that there is a body of law outlining legitimate citizen grievances, police agencies should eliminate the practices which have resulted in abuses. Public relations and community involvement programs will aid in shortening the bridge separating officers from others. Communication may prevent future clashes. Administrative handling of complaints is an alternative to civil litigation. Long range goals are better selection of officers and education of policemen.

CHAPTER EIGHTEEN

COMPLAINT HANDLING MECHANISMS

CIVIL litigation against policemen is one technique for handling complaints of abuse. A grievance is directed at the offending officer; recovery for losses is sought. A forum that is accustomed to dealing with conflicting testimony sifts the relevant and credible evidence and issues a decision that pertains specifically to the matter at hand. Even a defendant should recognize the beneficial aspects of such a process. He has an opportunity for exoneration. He may demand and receive a trial by a jury of his peers. If he is found liable, the amount of damages must be proven and linked to the facts. He can appeal the decision.

However, in taking a larger view of accusations against policemen, civil litigation does not appear to be the best solution for complainants, officers or the public. Courts are cumbersome, overburdened and snailpaced. Usually judges can only tailor remedies to the specific parties and not propose broad solutions. Similar abuses may not be prevented by this isolated handling of grievances. Any system to deal with these complaints should serve the following purposes: 1) investigate all complaints; 2) compensate individuals who had been injured; 3) discipline the offender, if necessary, or retrain the officer, if necessary, [or recommend such measures to appropriate authorities]; and 4) recommend changes in police practices to avoid future incidents. Several complaint handling procedures which are now in operation and have been widely discussed are the civilian review board, the ombudsman and internal review.

CIVILIAN REVIEW BOARD

Several cities have instituted civilian review boards to process police misconduct complaints. These boards are independent bodies that accept individual grievances and, after some form of investigation, either dismiss the accusation or recommend that departmental supervisors impose discipline. Such boards have existed in Philadelphia, New York City, Washington, Rochester, Minneapolis and York, Pennsylvania. Most of them arose in times of crises and quickly became defunct – largely due to police resistance. These boards did not displace preexisting complaint channels, such as in departments and courts, and did not levy punishments.

Police antagonism toward these boards stems from an assumption that their existence means that officers need to be watched over. Policemen resent being so singled out among public employees. They consider themselves professionals who do not need external guidance to properly perform their role. Also, they are skeptical that outsiders will understand the conditions under which officers function: rushing from incident to incident, grappling with a concentration of social ills and an infinite variety of situations requiring action.

Outside criticism of civilian review boards is that they are not independent of the police. Many boards have utilized police investigative services to examine official misconduct. Economy is the main factor here; however, the fairness of such an investigation is questioned. Also, collusion with agencies has been suspected because board decisions generally are secret. Exoneration or discipline of a policeman is not disclosed. Complainants rarely have an opportunity to face the officer whom they are accusing. An explanation or, if justified, an apology, would solve many misunderstandings.

Although not usually thought of in this context, the United States Supreme Court has been the most significant and effective civilian review of police practices throughout the nation. Its major decisions concerning law enforcement procedures have had the effect of substantially changing a greater number of abuses of police power than any other mechanism on the contemporary scene. For example, prolonged detention before arraignment has been denounced and its practice greatly reduced, confessions have been relegated to a less important position, and emphasis upon probable cause for arrest and search have diminished discriminatory seizure of persons and property.

A civilian review board that received and settled complaints fairly and promptly could serve a salutary purpose for citizens, policemen and the public. Individuals would have a forum for grievances before minor dissatisfactions grew into major accusations. For example, requests for expunction of records or explanation of police practices could be speedily handled. Funds should be allocated to the board for distribution to wronged claimants. The officer would benefit because the hazard of liability would be lessened and he would have a tribunal in which to defend himself from malicious and vengeful attacks by citizens. The time and expense of trial could be eliminated. Even if an administrative hearing were held, this would be an economical procedure compared with a trial. The public would gain because policemen would be away from duties for a shorter time in this process. The board would develop an expertise in police-citizen clashes that would ensure a balanced consideration of complaints and responses. Grievances would be funneled to a central agency that could review them and recommend changes in police practices.

OMBUDSMAN

The Scandinavian ombudsman system has received wide publicity recently. Variations have been instituted in a number of American jurisdictions; it is often proposed as a mechanism for dealing with police misconduct.

The ombudsman is an external critic of administration. In Scandinavia, he is usually a prominent jurist aided by a staff of lawyers and other specialists. His goal is the improvement of administration rather than the delving into redress of individual grievances. He does not conduct hearings but rather relies upon his own staff investigations to collect data. He receives complaints against any administrator or department informing him of questionable administrative policies that deserve scrutiny. He has broad access to agency files and sources. After an inquiry, he may reject baseless accusations or recommend corrective measures. Usually his conclusions are carefully explained to bureaucrats, complainants and the general public.

The ombudsman inspects all public services and is not limited to watching over police agencies. This comprehensive responsibility eliminates one of the prime antagonisms which police have felt toward civilian review boards: that officers have been singled out for opprobrium. Also, the broad vantage point of an ombudsman affords him insight into a better division of public functions among governmental agencies. Many duties have devolved upon the police without a rational examination of which department could better serve the public need. One example is contending with drunks. They are rarely so much a law enforcement problem as they are a social evil with which no one wants to cope. Many charges of police brutality arise from encounters with drunks. Officers are not equipped to deal with these unfortunates. Often force is used because of the unpleasantness and futility of this task.

Although the ombudsman concept is valuable in the realm of citizen complaints, it is a superstructure that does not solve immediate needs. The wronged person still needs a route for redress. Individual grievances must be heard and settled to avoid court adjudications.

INTERNAL REVIEW

Almost all police departments have a procedure for processing citizen complaints. Misbehaving officers can be disciplined, misconduct by other policemen can be deterred and reforms can be instituted. In many ways internal review is the most satisfactory form of complaint handling because it is at the seat of the trouble and the department itself can invoke effective censures. However, internal review is largely distrusted by outsiders and frequently does not provide appropriate remedies.

There are many reasons for community mistrust of internal review. Often the department responds with hostility to complainants. The filing of grievances may be discouraged by complex procedural formalities. Even the requirement of contacting the police themselves impedes some persons. Fear of retaliation, which is relevant to other complaint handling mechanisms, is perhaps more blatant to a person who comes directly to the agency than to one who contacts an external body. The department, whose member has been accused, investigates the charge. Bias is hard to eliminate, particularly if the unit to which the officer is assigned conducts the inquiry. The existence of a special internal investigative division strengthens the appearance of objectivety. Nondisclosure of the result of an inquiry cloaks it in a veil of secrecy which is difficult to dispel. If the public is to accept internal review as a valid technique for settling grievances and abolishing incendiary police practices, the procedure must be revealed and the outcome explained. Otherwise individuals will continue to seek court remedies. Full accounting of a dismissed accusation could publicly vindicate a policeman who behaved responsibly; invoking a punishment could placate citizen indignation over officer misconduct.

A significant criticism of internal review is that it is geared to enforcing department rules instead of redressing grievances. Token censure often is meted out for serious misconduct. Agency regulations are out of balance with citizen accusations. Unpolished shoes, tardiness and bad debts are fully treated in department manuals, but abuses of persons rarely warrant sanctions beyond those imposed for insubordination or gum chewing. The introduction of such regulations into court proceedings may be very embarassing to agencies that desire to handle complaints meaningfully.

Only if internal review wins public approval and projects an image of fairness can it hope to dislodge civil litigation as a method of redressing complaints. Also, department funds would have to be allocated for compensation of wronged individuals. This could be taken care of by a combination of an investigation by the police and settlement of damages by the city attorney or attorney general.

CONCLUSION

Four complaint handling mechanisms are civil litigation, civilian review boards, ombudsman and internal review. Each method has merit. Civil litigation is costly to everyone involved, including society, and is limited in its focus to the incident at hand. The other techniques, in addition to settling immediate grievances, may provide channels for police-community communication. From such contacts, all parties can work toward preventing future clashes.

CHAPTER NINETEEN

PERSONNEL SELECTION, EDUCATION AND LIABILITY-AVOIDANCE

THE police function is implemented through people. The quality of recruits in the coming years will determine the manner in which the public is served and how officers are regarded. Before law enforcement became so complex, anyone could pin on a badge and sally forth as a defender of society. Fine distinctions as to individual liberties and complicated investigations were not expected. A uniform was authority, force was power and confessions solved crimes. Different theories prevail today.

Personnel selection of yore focused upon physical prowess. Token evaluation was devoted to mental capacity and emotional traits. The hallmark of recruit selection in many agencies has been body dimensions. Height and blood pressure are easily taken; other qualities are not so simply measured. Physical fitness is necessary; however, a concentration on superman proportions led to dwelling upon the use of brawn rather than brain to overcome obstacles.

In the future, emphasis will be upon intelligence and psychological make-up. The police profession has been among the last to acknowledge intelligence as a prime criterion for recruiting. Examinations can predict whether a person has the mental potential for this occupation. He must also be qualified to obtain a college degree: an emerging demand for all officers. Psychiatric testing can flag emotionally unfit applicants before their entrance into the profession. Some attitudes can be molded by later education and psychological training, but other states of mind are too ingrained to be altered.

The tie between personnel selection and liability-avoidance is demonstrable. Those unsuited to exercise police power objectively and fairly will be barred. Candidates will not be accepted unless they have the capacity to comprehend the laws and match facts in the field to legitimate police practices. They must think their way through tricky legal distinctions and let deliberation substitute for impulse.

Selection of applicants is necessarily a long range program to revamp police into better people handlers. But what of the already commissioned officer who may be around for some years? He, too, should be comprehensively tested. If he is psychologically incompetent for contending with difficult human antagonisms, he should be shifted to assignments which are remote from confrontations. Since many intelligence and psychological examinations are available, supervisors may be faulted for not using these tools to weed out unfit applicants and to place inept officers in low-risk positions. Once a policeman is tested and found lacking in self-control or prone to use hands in lieu of head, employers and supervisors will be held responsible for not transferring him to nonincendiary duties.

EDUCATION

In the past few years a consensus has arisen that policemen must be educated. This realization accords with the generally higher level of education of the public and the extremely complex nature of modern law enforcement. The police desire for professionalism recognizes a college degree as part of its coveted image.

The first American policemen were citizen volunteers. This corps of law enforcers developed into full-time officers with little or no preparation. On the job experience gave them the know-how for their task: enforcing a few relatively simple laws in comparatively uncomplicated situations. The iceberg of civil rights had almost no tip showing. Authority was obvious and unquestioned. These officers performed the rough and ready work of upholding the law.

Only much later did training of policemen become the rule rather than the exception. Within the last few years a recognized need for training and federal grants for police purposes have made instruction available to most officers. These classes have consisted of police methods, department practices and a smattering of related matters. Schooling rarely exceeded weeks and virtually never lasted more than months. The necessity for training in arrest procedures, use of firearms and defensive driving is undeniable. Such instruction well may have satisfied the requirements for yesterday's policemen. Times have changed and so must the preparation of officers; vocational training is no longer sufficient.

To demand that today's policemen be educated is not to say that yesterday's officers were not fine troopers. Public expectations of law enforcers have altered drastically. Only a short while ago most arrests were for suspicion, for investigation or for vagrancy-type offenses. Now all such apprehensions are unconstitutional. Although probable cause has been the standard in arrests for two hundred years, increasingly the model filters down to the street. Those who do not follow the pattern block effective prosecutions and risk liability. Constitutional concepts are difficult to comprehend when seen in isolated criminal proceedings; much more is at stake than letting one culprit escape punishment. Study of government, history and law puts a particular case into a meaningful context. Much of a modern officer's time is spent in preventing annoyances from flaring into fights. Many such problems formerly were handled by families, schools and churches. But now it is the policeman who faces those strained by urban pressures and reeling under waves of future shock. An officer's innate skill with public relations needs the honing of the social sciences.

All of the education in the world may not keep an officer from embroilment in an alleged assault and battery. However, the knowledge that comes from a study of psychology may help him evade the irrational rage that explodes in clubbing a prisoner. Education engenders an ability to see beyond the momentary controversy to a balanced handling of crises.

An analogy to the military may be useful in looking at education of policemen. Few, if any, military leaders have not completed college. Their organizations acknowledge that benefits arising from this process are a prerequisite for responsibility. The government has long maintained military academies to educate future leaders. These facilities are four year colleges: not crash courses in battle readiness. Stress is placed upon learning to think. Many commentators have proposed a similar national academy for policemen. Such an academy, together with mushrooming college programs which award police science degrees, will provide opportunities for the education of all officers. Motivation to obtain college credit can be created by linking promotions and salary increases to educational accomplishments.

While field soldiers are not required to be educated, their role is clearly distinguishable from that of peace officers. Unsupervised discretion is rarely expected of nonranking soldiers. In police organizations, the greatest discretion, the hardest decisions and the speediest solving of problems are done by the patrolman. Supervisors can pause to consider appropriate moves and to seek guidance before acting. Usually they have time and space between themselves and irritating elements. The patrolman must swiftly choose his weapon. An educated patrolman is equipped with more than nightstick and gun; his background will aid him to understand the disturbed person he faces and will give him techniques for surmounting conflicts. The educated patrolman will not be easily led by the unschooled. Also, as these employees advance, the command ranks will be held by those with degrees.

Much of officers' resentment of court decisions comes from a lack of knowledge of the facts with which the judges grappled. Especially in ruling on constitutional questions, courts have examined law from a socio-historical perspective. Rulings on confessions and search warrants are much easier to accept if seen in the context of the mores of society. Education leads one to trace the development of the governmental process from that of noninterference in a simple pioneering frontier to that of maintaining a balance in a sophisticated, crowded environment. In order to cope with the latter, traditions of the former must be updated and transformed. Ideas, ideals and tolerances are not static.

Some particular facets of education that should result in liability avoidance are: 1) awareness of conflict-producing circumstances, 2) consciousness of personal motivations and aggressions, 3) methods of handling those overcome by tensions and 4) knowledge of law enforcement subjects. This listing demonstrates a leaning toward a liberal arts program. Knowledge of the humanities is required in order to deal with humanity. Courses that would lead to objectives 1), 2) and 3) are sociology, psychology and history, together with the basic components of a liberal arts curriculum. Category 4) would include police science matters such as legal aspects of law enforcement, philosophy of the police function and principles of administration. A balance between general classes and specialized subjects would give the student the particular tools for engaging in the profession of law enforcement and the vision to meet new challenges.

CONCLUSION

Personnel selection must take into consideration the evolving nature of police work. Intelligence and psychological traits are significant. No longer will rigid physical measurements alone determine recruit selection. In the future carefully chosen applicants will be college material as well as service-oriented individuals. A policeman who comprehends the basis for statutes and court decisions can better apply those laws in the street. He will think before he acts. An educated populace will demand and get educated policemen. Liability-avoidance is one objective of requiring that applicants be thoroughly screened for incompetence and that officers be educated.

APPENDIX

MANY constitutional provisions as well as state and federal statutes have been referred to throughout this book. Examples of such materials, and other legislation which is pertinent to civil litigation against officers, are listed in this appendix. The following data is not comprehensive, but is merely illustrative of some of the kinds of enactments which are currently effective.

1. AMENDMENTS TO THE UNITED STATES CONSTITUTION

Amendment I. Congress shall make no law respecting an establishment of religion, or prohibiting the free exercise thereof; or abridging the freedom of speech, or of the press; or the right of the people peaceably to assemble, and to petition the Government for a redress of grievances.

Amendment II. A well regulated Militia, being necessary to the security of a free state, the right of the people to keep and bear Arms, shall not be infringed.

Amendment III. No Soldier shall, in time of peace be quartered in any house, without the consent of the Owner, nor in time of war, but in a manner to be prescribed by law.

Amendment IV. The right of the people to be secure in their persons, houses, papers, and effects, against unreasonable searches and seizures, shall not be violated, and no Warrants shall issue, but upon probable cause, supported by Oath or affirmation, and particularly describing the place to be searched, and the persons or things to be seized.

Amendment V. No person shall be held to answer for a capital, or otherwise infamous crime, unless on a presentment or indictment of a Grand Jury, except in cases arising in the land or naval forces, or in the Militia, when in actual service in time of war or public danger; nor shall any person be subject for the same offense to be twice put in jeopardy of life or limb; nor shall be compelled in any Criminal Case to be a witness against himself; nor be deprived of life, liberty, or property, without due process of law; nor shall private property be taken for public use, without just compensation.

Amendment VI. In all criminal prosecutions, the accused shall enjoy the right to a speedy and public trial, by an impartial jury of the State and district wherein the crime shall have been committed, which district shall have been previously ascertained by law, and to be informed of the nature and cause of the accusation; to be confronted with the witnesses against him; to have compulsory process for obtaining Witnesses in his favor, and to have the Assistance of Counsel for his defence.

Amendment VII. In Suits at commonlaw, where the value in controversy shall exceed twenty dollars, the right of trial by jury shall be preserved, and no fact tried by a jury, shall be otherwise re-examined in any Court of the United States, than according to the rules of the common law.

Amendment VIII. Excessive bail shall not be required, nor excessive fines imposed, nor cruel and unusual punishments inflicted.

Amendment IX. The enumeration in the Constitution, of certain rights, shall not be construed to deny or disparage others retained by the people.

Amendment X. The powers not delegated to the United States by the constitution, nor prohibited by it to the States, are reserved to the States respectively, or to the people.

Amendment XI. The Judicial power of the United States shall not be construed to extend to any suit in law or equity, commenced or prosecuted against one of the United States by Citizens of another State, or by Citizens or Subjects of any Foreign State.

Amendment XII. The Electors shall meet in their respective states, and vote by ballot for President and Vice-President, one of whom, at least, shall not be an inhabitant of the same state with themselves; they shall name in their ballots the person voted for as President, and in distinct ballots the person voted for as Vice-President, and they shall make distinct lists of all persons voted for as President, and of all persons voted for as Vice-President, and of the number of votes for each, which lists they shall sign and certify, and transmit sealed to the seat of the government of the United States, directed to the President of the Senate; – The President of the Senate shall, in the presence of the Senate and House of Representatives, open all the certificates and the votes shall then be counted; – The person having the greatest number of votes for President, shall be the President, if such number be a majority of the whole number of Electors appointed; and if no person have such majority, then from the persons having the highest numbers not exceeding three on the list of those voted for as President, the House of Representatives shall choose immediately, by ballot, the President. But in choosing the President, the votes shall be taken by states, the representation from each state having one vote; a quorum for this purpose shall consist of a member or members from two-thirds of the States, and a majority of all the states shall be necessary to a choice. And if the House of Representatives shall not choose a President, whenever the right of choice shall devolve upon them, before the fourth day of March next following, then the Vice-President shall act as President, as in the case of the death or other constitutional disability of the President. The person having the greatest number of votes as Vice-President, shall be the Vice-President, if such number be a majority of the whole number of Electors appointed, and if no person have a majority, then from the two highest numbers on the list, the Senate shall choose the Vice-President; a quorum for the purpose shall consist of two-thirds of the whole number of Senators, and a majority of the whole number shall be necessary to a choice. But no person constitutionally ineligible to the office of President shall be eligible to that of Vice-President of the United States.

Amendment XIII. Section 1. Neither slavery nor involuntary servitude, except as a punishment for crime whereof the party shall have been duly convicted, shall exist within the United States, or any place subject to their jurisdictions.

Section 2. Congress shall have power to enforce this article by appropriate legislation.

Amendment XIV. Section 1. All persons born or naturalized in the United States, and subject to the jurisdiction thereof, are citizens of the United States and of the State wherein they reside. No state shall make or enforce any law which shall abridge the privileges or immunities of citizens of the United States; nor shall any State deprive any person of life, liberty, or property, without due process of law; nor deny to any person within its jurisdiction the equal protection of the laws.

Section 2. Representatives shall be apportioned among the several States according to their respective numbers, counting the whole number of persons in each State, excluding Indians not taxed. But when the right to vote at any election for the choice of electors for President and Vice President of the United States, Representatives in Congress, the Executive and Judicial officers of a State, or the members of the Legislature thereof, is denied to any of the male inhabitants of such State, being twenty-one years of age, and citizens of the United States, or in any way abridged, except for participation in rebellion, or other crime, the basis of representation therein shall be reduced in the proportion which the number of such male citizens shall bear to the whole number of male citizens twenty-one years of age in such State.

Section 3. No person shall be a Senator or Representative in

Congress, or elector of President and Vice President, or hold any office, civil or military, under the United States, or under any State, who, having previously taken an oath, as a member of Congress, or as an officer of the United States, or as a member of any State legislature, or as an executive or judicial officer of any State, to support the Constitution of the United States, shall have engaged in insurrection or rebellion against the same, or given aid or comfort to the enemies thereof. But Congress may by a vote of two-thirds of each House, remove such disability.

Section 4. The validity of the public debt of the United States, authorized by law, including debts incurred for payment of pensions and bounties for services in suppressing insurrection or rebellion, shall not be questioned. But neither the United States nor any State shall assume or pay any debt or obligation incurred in aid of insurrection or rebellion against the United States, or any claim for the loss of emancipation of any slave; but all such debts, obligations and claims shall be held illegal and void.

Section 5. The Congress shall have power to enforce, by appropriate legislation, the provisions of this article.

Amendment XV. Section 1. The right of citizens of the United States, to vote shall not be denied or abridged by the United States or by any State on account of race, color, or previous condition of servitude.

Section 2. The Congress shall have power to enforce this article by appropriate legislation.

Amendment XVI. The Congress shall have power to lay and collect taxes on incomes, from whatever source derived, without apportionment among the several states, and without regard to any census or enumeration.

Amendment XVII. The Senate of the United States shall be composed of two Senators from each state, elected by the people thereof, for six years; and each Senator shall have one vote. The electors in each state shall have the qualifications requisite for electors of the most numerous branch of the state legislatures.

When vacancies happen in the representation of any state in the Senate, the executive authority of such state shall issue writs of election to fill such vacancies: Provided, that the legislature of any state may empower the executive thereof to make temporary appointments until the people fill the vacancies by election as the legislature may direct.

This amendment shall not be so construed as to affect the election or term of any Senator chosen before it becomes valid as part of the Constitution.

Amendment XVIII. (Repealed December 5, 1933. See Amendment XXI, Section 1).

Amendment XIX. The right of citizens of the United States to vote shall not be denied or abridged by the United States or by any State on account of sex.

Congress shall have power to enforce this article by appropriate legislation.

Amendment XX. Section 1. The terms of the President and Vice President shall end at noon on the 20th day of January, and the terms of Senators and Representatives at noon on the 3d day of January, of the years in which such terms would have ended if this article had not been ratified; and the terms of their successors shall then begin.

Section 2. The Congress shall assemble at least once in every year, and such meeting shall begin at noon on the 3d day of January, unless they shall by law appoint a different day.

Section 3. If, at the time fixed for the beginning of the term of the President, the President elect shall have died, the Vice President elect shall become President. If a President shall not have been chosen before the time fixed for the beginning of his term, or if the President elect shall have failed to qualify, then the Vice President elect shall act as President until a President shall have qualified; and the Congress may by law provide for the case wherein neither a President elect nor a Vice President elect shall have qualified, declaring who shall then act as President, or the manner in which one who is to act shall be selected, and such person shall act accordingly until a President or Vice President shall have qualified.

Section 4. The Congress may by law provide for the case of the death of any of the persons from whom the House of Representatives may choose a President whenever the right of choice shall have devolved upon them, and for the case of the death of any of the persons from whom the Senate may choose a Vice President whenever the right of choice shall have devolved upon them.

Section 5. Sections 1 and 2 shall take effect on the 15th day of October following the ratification of this article.

Section 6. This article shall be inoperative unless it shall have been ratified as an amendment to the Constitution by the legislatures of three-fourths of the several States within seven years from the date of its submission.

Amendment XXI. Section 1. The eighteenth article of amendment to the Constitution of the United States is hereby repealed.

Section 2. The transportation or importation into any State, Territory, or possession of the United States for delivery or use therein of intoxicating liquors, in violation of the laws thereof, is hereby prohibited.

Section 3. This article shall be inoperative unless it shall have been ratified as an amendment to the Constitution by conventions in the several States, as provided in the Constitution, within seven years from the date of the submission hereof to the States by the Congress.

Amendment XXII. Section 1. No person shall be elected to the office of the President more than twice, and no person who has held the office of President, or acted as President, for more than two years of a term to which some other person was elected President shall be elected to the office of the President more than once. But this Article shall not apply to any person holding the office of President when this Article was proposed by the Congress, and shall not prevent any person who may be holding the office of President, or acting as President, during the term within which this Article become operative from holding the office of President or acting as President during the remainder of such term.

Section 2. This article shall be inoperative unless it shall have been ratified as an amendment to the Constitution by the legislatures of three-fourths of the several States within seven years from the date of its submission to the States by the Congress.

Amendment XXIII. Section 1. The District constituting the seat of Government of the United States shall appoint in such manner as the Congress may direct:

A number of electors of President and Vice President equal to the whole number of Senators and Representatives in Congress to which the District would be entitled if it were a State, but in no event more than the least populous State; they shall be in addition to those appointed by the States, but they shall be considered, for the purposes of the election of President and Vice President, to be electors appointed by a State; and they shall meet in the District and perform such duties as provided by the twelfth article of amendment.

Section 2. The Congress shall have power to enforce this article by appropriate legislation.

Amendment XXIV. Section 1. The right of citizens of the United States to vote in any primary or other election for President or Vice President, for electors for President or Vice

President, or for Senator or Representative in Congress, shall not be denied or abridged by the United States or any State by reason of failure to pay any poll tax or other tax.

Section 2. The Congress shall have power to enforce this article by appropriate legislation.

Amendment XXV. Section 1. In case of the removal of the President from office or of his death or resignation, the Vice President shall become President.

Section 2. Whenever there is a vacancy in the office of the Vice President, the President shall nominate a Vice President who shall take office upon confirmation by a majority vote of both Houses of Congress.

Section 3. Whenever the President transmits to the President pro tempore of the Senate and the Speaker of the House of Representatives his written declaration that he is unable to discharge the powers and duties of his office, and until he transmits to them a written declaration to the contrary, such powers and duties shall be discharged by the Vice President as Acting President.

Section 4. Whenever the Vice President and a majority of either the principal officers of the executive departments or of such other body as Congress may by law provide, transmit to the President pro tempore of the Senate and the Speaker of the House of Representatives their written declaration that the President is unable to discharge the powers and duties of his office, the Vice President shall immediately assume the powers and duties of the office as Acting President.

Thereafter, when the President transmits to the President pro tempore of the Senate and the Speaker of the House of Representatives his written declaration that no inability exists, he shall resume the powers and duties of his office unless the Vice President and a majority of either the principal officers of the executive department or of such other body as Congress may by law provide, transmit within four days to the President pro tempore of the Senate and the Speaker of the House of Representatives their written declaration that the President is unable to discharge the powers and duties of his office. Thereupon Congress shall decide the issue, assembling within forty-eight hours for that purpose if not in session. If the Congress, within twenty-one days after receipt of the latter written declaration, or, if Congress is not in session, within twenty-one days after Congress is required to assemble, determines by two-thirds vote of both Houses that the President is unable to discharge the powers and duties of his office, the Vice President shall continue to discharge the same as Acting President; otherwise, the President shall resume the powers and duties of his office.

2. BILL OF RIGHTS OF THE INDIANA CONSTITUTION

Constitution of Indiana, Art. 1, § § 1 to 37.

§ 1. Natural rights. – WE DECLARE, That all men are created equal; that they are endowed by their CREATOR with certain inalienable rights; that among these are life, liberty and the pursuit of happiness; that all power is inherent in the People; and that all free governments are, and of right ought to be, founded on their authority, and instituted for their peace, safety, and well-being. For the advancement of these ends, the People have, at all times, an indefeasible right to alter and reform their government.

§ 2. Right to worship. – All men, shall be secured in their natural right to worship Almighty God, according to the dictates of their own consciences.

§ 3. Freedom of thought. – No law shall, in any case whatever, control the free exercise and enjoyment of religious opinions, or interfere with the rights of conscience.

§ 4. No preference to any creed. – No preference shall be given, by law, to any creed, religious society, or mode of worship;

and no man shall be compelled to attend, erect, or support, any place of worship, or to maintain any ministry, against his consent.

§ 5. No religious test for office. – No religious test shall be required as a qualification for any office or trust or profit.

§ 6. No money for religious institutions. – No money shall be drawn from the treasury, for the benefit of any religious or theological institution.

§ 7. Competency of witness. – No person shall be rendered incompetent as a witness, in consequence of his opinions on matters of religion.

§ 8. Oath, how administered. – The mode of administering an oath or affirmation, shall be such as may be most consistent with, and binding upon the conscience of the person, to whom such oath or affirmation may be administered.

§ 9. Free speech and writing. – No law shall be passed, restraining the free interchange of thought and opinion, or restricting the right to speak, write, or print, freely, on any subject whatever: but for the abuse of that right, every person shall be responsible.

§ 10. The truth in libel. – In all prosecutions for libel, the truth of the matters alleged to be libellous may be given in justification.

§ 11. Unreasonable search or seizure. – The right of the people to be secure in their persons, houses, papers, and effects, against unreasonable search, or seizure, shall not be violated; and no warrant shall issue, but upon probable cause, supported by oath or affirmation, and particularly describing the place to be searched, and the person or thing to be seized.

§ 12. Courts open – Due course of law – Administration of justice. – All courts shall be open; and every man, for injury done to him in his person, property, or reputation, shall have remedy by due course of law. Justice shall be administered freely, and without purchase; completely, and without denial; speedily, and without delay.

§ 13. Rights of accused. – In all criminal prosecutions, the accused shall have the right to a public trial, by an impartial jury, in the county in which the offense shall have been committed; to be heard by himself and counsel; to demand the nature and cause of the accusation against him, and to have a copy thereof; to meet the witnesses face to face, and to have compulsory process for obtaining witnesses in his favor.

§ 14. Former jeopardy – Self-incrimination. – No person shall be put in jeopardy twice for the same offense. No person, in any criminal prosecution, shall be compelled to testify against himself.

§ 15. Unnecessary rigor prohibited. – No person arrested, or confined in jail, shall be treated with unnecessary rigor.

§ 16. Excessive bail, punishment, and penalties. – Excessive bail shall not be required. Excessive fines shall not be imposed. Cruel and unusual punishments shall not be inflicted. All penalties shall be proportioned to the nature of the offense.

§ 17. Bailable offenses. – Offenses, other than murder or treason, shall be bailable by sufficient sureties. Murder or treason shall not be bailable, when the proof is evident, or the presumption strong.

§ 18. Reformation as basis of penal code. – The penal code shall be founded on the principles of reformation, and not of vindictive justice.

§ 19. Jury in criminal cases – Right to determine law and facts. – In all criminal cases whatever, the jury shall have the right to determine the law and the facts.

§ 20. Trial by jury inviolate in civil cases. – In all civil cases, the right of trial by jury shall remain inviolate.

§ 21. Compensation for services or property. – No man's particular services shall be demanded, without just compensation. No man's property shall be taken by law, without just compensation; nor, except in case of the State, without such compensation first assessed and tendered.

§ 22. Exemption – Imprisonment for debt. – The privilege of the debtor to enjoy the necessary comforts of life, shall be recognized by wholesome laws, exempting a reasonable amount of property from seizure or sale for the payment of any debt or liability hereafter contracted; and there shall be no imprisonment for debt, except in case of fraud.

§ 23. Privileges equal. – The General Assembly shall not grant to any citizen, or class of citizens, privileges or immunities which, upon the same terms, shall not equally belong to all citizens.

§ 24. Ex post facto laws – Laws impairing obligations of contract. – No ex post facto law, or law impairing the obligation of contracts, shall ever be passed.

§ 25. Taking effect of laws. – No law shall be passed, the taking effect of which shall be made to depend upon any authority, except as provided in this Constitution.

§ 26. Suspension of laws. – The operation of the laws shall never be suspended, except by the authority of the General Assembly.

§ 27. Suspension of habeas corpus. – The privilege of the writ of habeas corpus shall not be suspended, except in case of rebellion or invasion; and then, only if the public safety demand it.

§ 28. Treason. – Treason against the State shall consist only in levying war against it, and in giving aid and comfort to its enemies.

§ 29. Proof in treason. – No person shall be convicted of treason, except on the testimony of two witnesses to the same overt act, or upon his confession in open court.

§ 30. Effect of conviction. – No conviction shall work corruption of blood, or forfeiture of estate.

§ 31. Right to assemble, instruct and petition. – No law shall restrain any of the inhabitants of the State from assembling together in a peaceable manner, to consult for their common good; nor from instructing their representatives; nor from applying to the General Assembly for redress of grievances.

§ 32. Right to bear arms. – The people shall have a right to bear arms, for the defense of themselves and the State.

§ 33. Military subject to civil power. – The military shall be kept in strict subordination to the civil power.

§ 34. Restrictions upon soldiers. – No soldier shall, in time of peace, be quartered in any house, without the consent of the owner; nor, in time of war, but in a manner to be prescribed by law.

§ 35. No titles of nobility, nor hereditary distinctions. – The General Assembly shall not grant any title of nobility, nor confer hereditary distinctions.

§ 36. Emigration free. – Emigration from the State shall not be prohibited.

§ 37. Slavery prohibited. – There shall be neither slavery, nor involuntary servitude, within the State, otherwise than for the punishment of crimes, whereof the party shall have been duly convicted. No indenture of any Negro or Mulatto, made and executed out of the bounds of the State, shall be valid within the State.

3. WAIVER OF SOVEREIGN IMMUNITY WHEN INSURED

New Hampshire Revised Statutes Annotated § *412:3.*

§ 412:3. Procured by Governmental Agency. It shall be lawful for the state or any municipal subdivision thereof, including any county, city, town, school district, supervisory union or other district, to procure the policies of insurance described in section 1 of this chapter. In any action against the state or any municipal subdivision thereof to enforce liability on account of a risk so insured against, the insuring company or state or municipal subdivision thereof, shall not be allowed to plead as a defense immunity from liability for damages resulting from the performance of governmental functions, and its liability shall be determined as in the case of a private corporation. Provided, however, that liability in any such case shall not exceed the limits of coverage specified in the policy of insurance, and the court shall abate any verdict in any such action to the extent that it exceeds such policy limit.

4. ALLOWANCE OF LIMITED AMOUNT OF LIABILITY

General Statutes of North Carolina § *143-291.*

Tort claims against State Departments and Agencies. § 143-291. Industrial Commission constituted a court to hear and determine claims; damages. –The North Carolina Industrial Commission is hereby constituted a court for the purpose of hearing and passing upon tort claims against the State Board of Education, the State Highway Commission, and all other departments, institutions and agencies of the State. The Industrial Commission shall determine whether or not each individual claim arose as a result of a negligent act of any officer, employee, involuntary servant or agent of the State while acting within the scope of his office, employment, service, agency or authority, under circumstances where the State of North Carolina, if a private person, would be liable to the claimant in accordance with the laws of North Carolina. If the Commission finds that there was such negligence on the part of an officer, employee, involuntary servant or agent of the State while acting within the scope of his office, employment, service, agency or authority, which was the proximate cause of the injury and that there was no contributory negligence on the part of the claimant or the person in whose behalf the claim is asserted, the Commission shall determine the amount of damages which the claimant is entitled to be paid, including medical and other expenses, and by appropriate order direct the payment of such damages by the department, institution or agency concerned, but in no event shall the amount of damages awarded exceed the sum of twenty thousand dollars ($20,000.00).

5. WAIVER OF SOVEREIGN IMMUNITY

R.C.W.A. (Washington)* § § *4.92.090 and 4.96.010.

RCWA 4.92.090 Tortious conduct of the state – Liability for damages. The state of Washington, whether acting in its governmental or proprietary capacity, shall be liable for damages arising out of its tortious conduct to the same extent as if it were a private person or corporation.

RCWA 4.96.010 Tortious conduct of political subdivisions, municipal corporations and quasi municipal corporations – Liability for damages. All political subdivisions, municipal corporations, and quasi municipal corporations of the state, whether acting in a governmental or proprietary capacity, shall be liable for damages arising out of their tortious conduct, or the tortious conduct of their officers, agents or employees to the same extent as if they were a private person or corporation: *Provided,* That the filing within the time allowed by law of any claim required shall be a condition precedent to the maintaining of any action. The laws specifying the content for such claims shall be liberally construed so that substantial compliance therewith will be deemed satisfactory.

6. COMPROMISE AND SETTLEMENT OF TORT CLAIMS

Code of Iowa 1971 § 613 A.9.

§ 613 A.9. Compromise and settlement. The governing body of any municipality may compromise, adjust and settle tort claims against the municipality, its officers, employees and agents, for damages under section 613 A.2 [actions within the scope of employment] or 613 A.8 [defense of officers and employees] and may appropriate money for the payment of amounts agreed upon.

7. PURCHASE OF LIABILITY INSURANCE

South Dakota C. L. 1967 § 7-12-26.1.

SDCL 1967 § 7-12-26.1. Purchase of liability insurance for county peace officers-Premiums – Liability limits. – The board of county commissioners shall have power to purchase and pay premiums on insurance covering and insuring county peace officers, including sheriff, which insurance shall insure against personal liability as a result of errors and omissions in the performance of official duties. The board of county commissioners shall purchase and pay premiums on such insurance for deputies and employees of those county peace officers for which the board may determine the insurance necessary. The premiums shall be paid from the county general fund. Minimum liability limits for such insurance necessary, shall be fixed by the attorney general.

8. PARTICULAR PROVISION REGARDING MOTOR VEHICLE INSURANCE

West Virginia Code of 1961 § 494 (6).

§ 494 (6) W. Va. Code of 1961. Public Liability, Bodily Injury Liability and Property Damage Liability Insurance by Municipalities. – The governing body of every municipal corporation within this state is hereby expressly authorized the expend public funds for the purchase of public liability, bodily injury liability and property damage liability insurance policies for the protection of such municipalities, its officers, agents and employees against the negligent operation of all motor vehicles owned by such municipality, and against negligence in the operation of any proprietary or commercial function of such municipality.

9. TIME LIMITATIONS ON LAWSUITS

Revised Codes of Montana 1947 § 93-2608.

Rev. Codes of Mont. 1947 (Repl. Vol. 7 1964) § 93-2608. One-year limitation. Within one year:

1. An action against a sheriff, or other officer, for the escape of a prisoner, arrested or imprisoned on civil process.

2. An action against a municipal corporation for damages or injuries to property caused by a mob or riot; or by a municipal corporation for the violation of any city or town ordinance.

3. An action against an officer or officer de facto, to recover any goods, wares, merchandise, or other property seized by any such officer in his official capacity as tax collector, or to recover the price or value of any goods, wares, merchandise, or other personal property so seized, or for damages for the seizure, detention, sale of, or injury to any goods, wares, merchandise, or other personal property seized, or for damages done to any person or property in making any such seizure.

10. TIME LIMITATIONS ON LAWSUITS

Arkansas Statutes 1947 Annotated Chapter 2, § 37-201.

§ 37-201. Actions which must be brought within one year – Tort action. – The following actions shall be commenced within one year after the cause of action shall accrue, and not after: first, all special actions on the case, actions for criminal conversation, alienation of affection, assault and battery and false imprisonment; second, all actions for words spoken slandering the character of another; third, all words spoken whereby special damages are sustained.

11. COSTS AND ATTORNEY FEES IN SUIT AGAINST OFFICER

Utah C. A. 1953 § *78-11-10.*

Actions against officers – Costs and attorney's fees. – Before any action may be filed against any sheriff, constable, peace officer, state road officer, or any other person charged with the duty of enforcement of the criminal laws of this state, or service of civil process, when such action arises out of, or in the course of the performance of his duty, or in any action upon the bond of such officer, the proposed plaintiff, as a condition precedent thereto, shall prepare and file with, and at the time of filing the complaint in any such action, a written undertaking with at least two sufficient sureties in an amount to be fixed by the court, conditioned upon the diligent prosecution of such action, and, in the event judgment in the said cause shall be against the plaintiff, for the payment to the defendant of all costs and expenses that may be awarded against such plaintiff, including a reasonable attorney's fee to be fixed by the court. In any such action, the prevailing party therein shall, in addition to an award of costs as otherwise provided, recover from the losing party therein such sum as counsel fees as shall be allowed by the court. The official bond of any such officer shall be liable for any such costs and attorney fees.

12. DUTY TO ARREST

Wyoming Statutes § *7-12 and 13.*

§ 7-12. Crimes and offenses committed in presence of officer – Duty to arrest; prisoner to be taken forthwith to magistrate. – It shall be the duty of every sheriff, marshal, policeman, constable and other peace officer promptly, and at the time and without warrant, to arrest any person who in his presence shall be found violating any law of the State of Wyoming, and forthwith to take such person before the nearest magistrate having jurisdiction of such offense, and forthwith before such magistrate to make complaint on oath of such person concerning such offense.

§ 7-13. Same – Penalty for refusal to arrest; proceedings for ouster from office. – Any such sheriff, marshal, policemen, constable or other peace officer, who fails or refuses to arrest any person committing any offense in his presence as above required, may be complained of under oath concerning such failure or refusal, before the district court of the county within which he exercises his office, by any voter of such county, and if found guilty of such failure or refusal he shall by the judgment of such court in such proceeding be ousted from his office, and such office shall thereby become vacant.

13. ARRESTS WITHOUT WARRANT; LIABILITY

15 M.R.S.A. (Maine) § 704.

§ 704. Arrests without warrant; liability. Every sheriff, deputy sheriff, constable, city or deputy marshal, or police officer shall arrest and detain persons found violating any law of the State or any legal ordinance or bylaw of a town until a legal warrant can be obtained and may arrest and detain such persons against whom a warrant has been issued though the officer does not have the warrant in his possession at the time of the arrest, and they shall be entitled to legal fees for such service; but if, in so doing, he acts wantonly or oppressively, or detains a person without a warrant longer than is necessary to procure it, he shall be liable to such person for the damages suffered thereby.

14. WHEN FORCE NOT UNLAWFUL

21 Oklahoma Statutes Annotated § 643.

§ 643. Force against another not unlawful, when – Self-defense

– Defense of Property. To use or to attempt to offer to use force or violence upon or toward the person of another is not unlawful in the following cases:

1. When necessarily committed by a public officer in the performance of any legal duty; or by any other person assisting him or acting by his direction.

2. When necessarily committed by any person in arresting one who has committed any felony, and delivering him to a public officer competent to receive him in custody.

3. When committed either by the party about to be injured, or by any other person in his aid or defense, in preventing or attempting to prevent an offense against his person, or any trespass or other unlawful interference with real or personal property in his lawful possession; provided the force or violence used is not more than sufficient to prevent such offense.

4. When committed by a parent or the authorized agent of any parent, or by any guardian, master or teacher, in the exercise of a lawful authority to restrain or correct his child, ward, apprentice or scholar; provided restraint or correction has been rendered necessary by the misconduct of such child, ward, apprentice or scholar, or by his refusal to obey the lawful command of such parent or authorized agent or guardian, master or teacher, and the force or violence used is reasonable in manner and moderate in degree.

5. When committed by a carrier of passengers, or the authorized agents or servants of such carrier, or by any person assisting them at their request, in expelling from any carriage, railroad car, vessel, or other vehicle, any passenger who refuses to obey a lawful and reasonable regulation prescribed for the conduct of passengers, if such vehicle has first been stopped and the force and violence used is not more than sufficient to expel the offending passenger, with a reasonable regard to his personal safety.

6. When committed by any person in preventing an idiot, lunatic, insane person or other person of unsound mind, including persons temporarily or partially deprived of reason, from committing an act dangerous to himself or to another, or enforcing such restraint as is necessary for the protection of his

person or for his restoration to health, during such period only as shall be necessary to obtain legal authority for the restraint or custody of his person.

15. COUNSEL FOR POLICE OFFICERS

Hawaii Statutes § 52-3 and 4.

§ 52-3 Police officers, counsel for. Whenever any police officer is prosecuted for any crime or sued in any civil cause for acts done in the performance of his duty as a police officer, he shall be represented and defended,

(1) In the criminal proceeding by an attorney to be employed and paid by the board of supervisors or city council of the county in which the officer is serving, and

(2) In the civil case by the corporation counsel or county attorney, as the case may be, of the county in which the police officer is serving.

§ 52-4. Determination whether acts were in scope of duty. The determination of whether the acts of the police officer, for which he is being prosecuted or sued, were done in the performance of his duty, so as to entitle him to be represented by counsel provided by the county, shall be made by the police commission of the county after consultation with the county attorney or the corporation counsel who may make a recommendation to the commission with respect thereto if he so desires, and the determination shall be conclusive for this purpose only.

16. INDEMNIFICATION OF OFFICERS

Revised Statutes Nebraska 1943 § 23-1716.

§ 23-1716. Section 1. If any legal action shall be brought against any municipal police officer or constable, or county sheriff or deputy sheriff, based upon the conduct of such official while in the performance of law enforcement duties, the municipality or county which employs such official shall defend such official against such action and if final judgment is rendered against such official then such municipality or county shall pay such judgment in his behalf and shall have no right to restitution from such official. Any municipality or county shall have the right to purchase insurance to indemnify itself in advance against the possibility of such loss under the provisions of this section, and the insurance company shall have no right of subrogation against the official.

17. ACTING UNDER UNCONSTITUTIONAL LAW

California Gov. Code § *820.6.*

§ 820.6. Acting under unconstitutional, invalid or inapplicable enactments. If a public employee acts in good faith, without malice, and under the apparent authority of an enactment that is unconstitutional, invalid or inapplicable, he is not liable for an injury caused thereby except to the extent that he would have been liable had the enactment been constitutional, valid and applicable.

18. EXEMPTION OF SUPERIOR

California Gov. Code § *820.8.*

§ 820.8. Acts or omissions of others. Except as otherwise provided by statute, a public employee is not liable for an injury caused by the act or omission of another person. Nothing in this section exonerates a public employee from liability for injury proximately caused by his own negligent or wrongful act or omission.

19. FEDERAL CIVIL RIGHTS STATUTES

§ *1983. Civil action for deprivation of rights*

§ 1983. Every person who, under color of any statute, ordinance, regulation, custom, or usage, of any State or Territory, subjects, or causes to be subjected, any citizen of the United States or other person within the jurisdiction thereof to the deprivation of any rights, privileges, or immunities secured by the Constitution and laws, shall be liable to the party injured in an action at law, suit in equity, or other proper proceeding for redress.

§ *1985. Conspiracy to interfere with civil rights – Preventing officer from performing duties*

§ 1985. (1) If two or more persons in any State or Territory conspire to prevent, by force, intimidation, or threat, any person from accepting or holding any office, trust, or place of confidence under the United States, or from discharging any duties thereof; or to induce by like means any officer of the United States to leave any State, district, or place, where his duties as an officer are required to be performed, or to injure him in his person or property on account of his lawful discharge of duties of his office, or while engaged in the lawful discharge thereof, or to injure his property so as to molest, interrupt, hinder, or impede him in the discharge of his official duties;

§ 1985. (2) Obstructing justice; intimidating party, witness, or juror. If two or more persons in any State or Territory conspire to deter, by force, intimidation, or threat, any party or witness in any court of the United States from attending such court, or from testifying to any matter pending therein, freely, fully, and truthfully, or to injure such party or witness in his person or property on account of his having so attended or testified, or to influence the verdict, presentment, or indictment of any grand or petit juror in any such court, or to injure such juror; in his person or property on account of any verdict, presentment, or indictment lawfully assented to by him, or of his being or having been such juror; or if two or more persons conspire for the purpose of impeding, hindering, obstructing, or defeating, in any manner, the due course of justice in any State or Territory, with intent to deny to any citizen the equal protection of the laws, or to injure him or his property for lawfully enforcing, or attempting to enforce, the right of any person, or class of persons, to the equal protection of the laws;

§ 1985. (3) Depriving persons of rights or privileges. If two or more persons in any State or Territory conspire or go in disguise on the highway or on the premises of another, for the purpose of depriving, either directly or indirectly, any person or class of persons of the equal protection of the laws, or of equal privileges and immunities under the laws; or for the purpose of preventing or hindering the constituted authorities of any State or Territory from giving or securing to all persons within such State or Territory the equal protection of the laws; or if two or more persons conspire to prevent by force, intimidation, or threat, any citizen who is lawfully entitled to vote, from giving his support or advocacy in a legal manner, toward or in favor of the election of any lawfully qualified person as an elector for President or Vice President, or as a Member of Congress of the United States; or to injure any citizen in person or property on account of such support or advocacy; in any case of conspiracy set forth in this section, if one or more persons engaged therein do, or cause to be done, any act in furtherance of the object of such conspiracy, whereby another is injured in his person or property, or deprived of having and exercising any right or privilege of a citizen of the United States, the party so injured or deprived may have an action for the recovery of damages, occasioned by such injury or deprivation, against any one or more of the conspirators.

GLOSSARY

admission: The voluntary acknowledgement made by a plaintiff or defendant either orally, in writing or by conduct as to the existence or truth of certain facts.

affirm: The ratifying or upholding by a higher court of a judgment by a lower court or board.

affirmative defense: New matter constituting a defense; not simply a denial of plaintiff's allegation but the assertion of a positive statement which must be proven by defendant. For example, contributory negligence, consent or waiver.

allege (allegation): To declare or assert without proof; to state positively.

answer: A pleading by defendant setting up his defense.

appellate court: A court to which a matter is appealed from a lower court or administrative board; facts are determined in the trial court or board hearing, and decisions in an appellate court are based upon an application of the law to such facts.

assert (assertion): See allege.

assumption of the risk: A defense to a negligence claim; allegation that plaintiff knew of the danger and intelligently acquiesced in it.

bench: The seat occupied by a judge in court; also the court itself.

burden of proof: The duty of the person who brings a lawsuit to establish the elements of his case by the amount of proof demanded by law. In criminal cases the accused is presumed to be innocent until his guilt is established, and the burden of proof is upon the prosecutor to establish, beyond a reasonable doubt, every element of the offense of which the accused is charged. In civil cases the plaintiff has the burden of proving the elements of his case by the preponderance of the evidence (greater weight of the evidence). In an affirmative defense the burden of proof on the one who asserts the defense is to establish the elements of the defense.

cause of action: The right to bring a lawsuit; the right to relief in court; matters about which a court will render a judgment (such matters are said to be actionable).

civil action: A lawsuit initiated to recover for the infraction of a private or civil right; any lawsuit which is not criminal.

civil death: A consequence of conviction of certain crimes which means that the person is regarded as dead in law and can perform no legal function.

civil rights: Guarantees which are contained in constitutional and statutory law.

color of law: Under pretense of law including but not limited to under authority of law; clothed with the authority of law regardless of whether conduct is legal or illegal.

common law: Law derived from court decisions, including court decisions and statutes of England before the American revolution; a term used to distinguish case law from statutes (the term is defined by statute in many states).

complainant: One who applies to the courts for legal redress; see plaintiff.

complaint: The first or initiatory pleading on the part of plaintiff.

compensatory damages: A monetary amount that is demanded in a complaint to recover for injury sustained; an amount which will replace the loss caused by the injury or wrong.

concurring opinion: A statement by a judge who agrees with the general result of the decision by the majority of the court but who disapproves some aspects of the majority opinion such as the grounds or the reasoning.

contend (contention): See allege.

contributory negligence: An affirmative defense to a negligence claim alleging that plaintiff departed from the standard of conduct of a reasonable man and that such departure was a cause of plaintiff's injury.

count: A part of a complaint which alleges a cause of action.

court: A person or persons appointed or elected to conduct trials; a place where trials are held.

damages: Monetary compensation which may be recovered in the courts by any person who has suffered loss or injury to his person, property or rights through the unlawful act or omission or negligence of another; see compensatory damages and punitive, or exemplary, damages.

decision: A judgment or holding given by a court in settlement of a controversy.

defendant (respondent): Party who is sued.

deposition: A statement made by a party or a witness in response to questions; statements made under oath and pursuant to court rules but not taken in court; written answers under oath which are usable at a trial under certain circumstances, such as for impeachment (discrediting) of a witness.

directed verdict: Decision by the court that plaintiff has not produced evidence which is sufficient in law to sustain a judgment in his favor; in ruling on a defendant's motion for directed verdict a judge will accept as true every fact which plaintiff's evidence tends to prove and every favorable conclusion which might reasonably be inferred from plaintiff's evidence, and the judge will only rule for defendant if the judge decides that plaintiff's evidence is not sufficient to sustain a verdict for plaintiff.

dissenting opinion: A statement by a judge which announces his disagreement with the conclusion of the majority of the court and expounds his views.

due process of law: Law according to the regular course of administration through judicial proceedings; a concept having to do with fundamental fairness.

enjoin: See injunction.

expunction (expunging): To strike out; delete; cancel.

governmental immunity: See sovereign immunity.

gross negligence: Failure to use that amount of care which even a careless person would use; more than ordinary inadvertence or inattention but less than conscious indifference to consequences; an extreme departure from the ordinary standard of care; between ordinary negligence and willful, wanton and reckless activity.

holding: Decision of a court.

indemnification: Protection from loss; compensation of a person for damages or loss incurred.

indictment: A written accusation by a grand jury charging a person with the commission of a crime.

information: A written accusation by a competent public official, usually a district attorney or a United States Attorney, charging a person with the commission of a crime.

injunction (enjoin): A court order forbidding a defendant from doing some act which he is threatening to do or restraining him from the continuance of an act because it is unjust or illegal toward plaintiff and plaintiff cannot be compensated adequately by a monetary award.

instructions to the jury: A statement by the judge to the jury informing them of the law applicable to the case.

intent (in civil cases): Doing of a voluntary act which to a substantial certainty will injure another.

interrogatories: A series of questions asked of a witness or a party to a lawsuit.

judgment: A judicial decision.

jurisdiction: The power of a court to hear and determine the subject matter in controversy between parties to a suit.

jurisprudence: The science or philosophy of law; a system of laws.

liable (liability): Legally obligated; responsible.

litigation: The act or process of carrying out a lawsuit.

loss: Injury or damage that is the basis for a claim.

magistrate: A judge of a lower court, such as justice of the peace or judge of a police court.

malfeasance: Wrongdoing in handling public affairs.

misfeasance: Doing a lawful act in an unlawful manner so as to infringe upon the rights of another.

mores: Folkways; traditional customs of a social group that through general observance become to have the force of law.

motion to dismiss: A request by one party to send a matter out of court without further consideration. In ruling on a defendant's motion to dismiss a plaintiff's complaint, the court will accept as true any allegations by plaintiff that are stated in correct legal form. If the motion is overruled, of course, plaintiff will have to prove the allegation before prevailing.

negligence: The omission to do something which a reasonable man, guided by the usual considerations which ordinarily regulate human affairs, would do, or the doing of something which a reasonable and prudent man would not do under similar circumstances.

nolle prosequi: A formal entry upon the record by plaintiff in a civil suit or the prosecutor in a criminal case that he will no longer prosecute the case either as to some counts or some defendants or altogether.

nolo contendere: A plea in a criminal case which has the same effect as a guilty plea but is not to be used as an admission in any other case, such as in a civil suit based upon the same incident.

nonfeasance: Failure to perform a duty.

opinion: Statement by a judge of the decision reached in a case, explaining the law as applied to the case and detailing the reasons upon which the judgment is based.

ordinary negligence: See negligence.

petition: See complaint.

petitioner: See plaintiff, complainant

plaintiff (petitioner; complainant): Person who brings a civil lawsuit.

pleadings: The formal allegations by the parties to a lawsuit of their claims and defenses.

precedent: A court decision that serves as an example or authority for future cases.

presumption: The inference that a fact exists based upon the proved existence of other facts. Rebuttable presumption is one which holds good until it is invalidated by proof or a stronger presumption. Conclusive presumption is one which cannot be overcome by any proof.

prima facie case: One which is established by sufficient evidence and can be overthrown only by rebutting evidence from the opposing side.

proximate cause: That which, in a natural and continuous sequence, unbroken by any efficient cause, produces the injury, and without which the result would not have occurred.

punitive (or exemplary) damages: A monetary amount that is demanded in a complaint to punish defendant for his evil behavior; money awarded when the wrong done to plaintiff is aggravated by violence, oppression, malice or wicked conduct of defendant.

quash: To dismiss or set aside, as an indictment.

recovery: The amount of the judgment awarded.

redress: Satisfaction for an injury sustained.

relief: The end to which litigation is directed; what plaintiff seeks in a lawsuit.

remedy: The means by which violation of a right is prevented or compensated for; the end to which litigation is directed.

reparation: Redress of an injury; amends for a wrong inflicted.

respondent: See defendant.

reversed: A term used by appellate courts in setting aside the judgment of the lower court or board.

sanction: An authorization of anything; something that produces obedience to a law such as a penalty for breaking it or reward for carrying it out.

self-defense: An affirmative defense or excuse for use of force in resisting an attack on the person.

sovereign immunity (governmental immunity): An exemption from being sued which applies to a governmental unit or official or both.

subpoena: A court order requiring a person to attend court at a particular time and place as a witness.

summary judgment: A decision upon the law applicable to a case after a finding by the court that there are no factual issues in dispute and the case is subject to a ruling only upon questions of law.

surety: A guarantee against loss or damage; a guarantor.

tort: Private injury for which suit is brought by the injured party; legal wrong committed upon a person or property independent of a contract.

tortfeasor: One who commits a tort.

unavoidable accident: An affirmative defense that an accident was inevitable.

venue: The place at which a trial will be held. A change of venue is a transfer of a case from one location to another. Usually such transfer is made when there may be prejudice of the judge or jury if the case is not moved to a different place.

verdict: The formal finding of a jury on the matter submitted to them in a trial; a decision; judgment.

voir dire: [To speak the truth] An examination, by a judge or an attorney, of a juror or a witness to determine whether he is competent to sit as a member of a jury or to testify as a witness. Some reasons why a witness would be found to be incompetent are lack of expertise, age of a child, mental condition of a deranged person or coercion. Some reasons why a juror would be found to be incompetent are close relationship to a party in a lawsuit, prejudice or prior knowledge of events.

waiver: Voluntary relinquishment of a known right.

wrongful death: A theory for a lawsuit alleging that defendant's acts caused the death of a person and that defendant is liable for damages because of causing death.

INDEX OF CASES

Page

A

B

N

O

P

SUBJECT INDEX

D

P

Q

R